With Best wishes
from
Carae Cooper.

Crypts 1977.

Ch. Gipsy Duke

THE NEWFOUNDLAND

Edited by
CAROL COOPER

Published by
THE NEWFOUNDLAND CLUB

THIS BOOK . . . . .

Is for Cindy, who was the start of it,
and for the generations of dedicated
breeders who made her, and all the other
"Gentle Bears" possible.

Foreword

I am delighted to present "The Newfoundland". I wish to congratulate the Editor Mrs Carol Cooper on her wonderful work on
publishing this book. We have never had a complete book on this breed
in our own country, since the founding of the Newfoundland Club in
1886, and it coincides with the celebrations of our ninetieth
anniversary.

Many members have contributed articles and Mrs Cooper has put a
great deal of time and work into research for this book. Every member
of our club and owner of a Newfoundland should have the book as a
"must" in their doggy library.

Thank you, Mrs Carol Cooper.

May Roberts (President)
Newfoundland Club

Acknowledgments

This book has been created by people who love Newfoundlands. I hope that it will help new owners to enjoy and care for their dogs, as well as interest and perhaps widen the understanding of those who already own dogs of this breed.

My gratitude to those who have contributed to the book is enormous. Without their help it would not have been written. All gave their time and knowledge freely, but I would like to make a special mention of Mrs Esther Denham. She is more than fully occupied with a busy veterinary practice and yet found time to write a very long and detailed chapter.

In addition to correcting the manuscript, Mrs Roberts and Mrs Handley have also given me a great deal of help with information and pictures of early dogs and their breeders.

To those who have lent me photographs, sometimes very precious ones, and often at their own expense, thank you. I am especially indebted to Mrs Burgess of Thomas Fall's who, in the middle of moving house, found the time to search through her records and provide me with some very old and interesting prints.

The Newfoundland Club is very fortunate in having the professional services of Tod Handley as over-all editor of their book. He has been most generous with his time, and I am grateful for his silent emendations.

My thanks too, to the printers who have made this book. Their enthusiasm has been encouraging and their technical advice invaluable.

The cost of publishing any kind of book today is high and we have always felt that "The Newfoundland" should be produced to a reasonable standard, or not at all. Many Club members have contributed to the Book Fund to make this possible, either out of their own pockets or by organising fund-raising activities. I hope they feel their efforts have been worth-while, for without their help the book would never have reached the printer.

Lastly, the book would never have been completed without the help and support of Jeanne Davies. As Club Secretary, she is also the unofficial Club Archivist, and she has been bombarded with requests for information, which she has never failed to provide. She has also read the manuscript and made many helpful suggestions. I am deeply grateful to her.

Carol Cooper
Brecon
September 1976

Contents

The Eslington Newfoundland by Thomas Bewick

CHAPTER ONE

Origins and History

"His foure feet (should be) spatious, full and round, and closed together to the cley, like a Water Ducke, for they being his oars to rowe him in the Water, having that shape, will carry his body away faster."

(Gervase Markham writing of the Water Dog in 1621)

To the student of canine history, one of the most attractive aspects of the Newfoundland is that relatively little is known of his early origins. This offers opportunities for research, with the chance that something completely new may be unearthed about the breed. The ancient and well-documented lineage of the Saluki or the Pekinese does not belong to the Newfoundland.

It now seems certain that the Newfoundland as we know him today did not originate in North America. Archaeological surveys made from the far north of the continent down to Mexico show that all the indigenous dogs were Spitz in type. They ranged from Husky-like dogs in the north to smaller, shorter-coated dogs in the south. They all shared the common features of small, pointed ears and curled tails. Heads were wedge-shaped with pointed muzzles.

There is considerable evidence that the North American Indians bred some of their dogs to wolves. The resulting progeny, improved in size and

Newfoundland

with thick, weather-resisting coats, were highly prized as draught animals, pulling loads through the snow in winter, and back-packing in the summer season. It should be remembered that the horse was unknown before the Spanish invasion of South America. The Indians also used the dogs for hunting game and in many cases they were eaten as well.

In a survey carried out by Glover M. Allen, skulls of dogs from Kodiak Island were examined. They dated from approximately the beginning of the Christian era to 1783, and differed very little from modern Greenland Eskimo dog skulls. There was no suggestion of any mastiff-like characteristics. Other surveys in North America suggest that this pattern is consistent throughout the country, the only variations being in size.

10

The Beothuck Indians

These are thought to be the first humans to have inhabited Newfoundland. It would be satisfactory to be able to record that these gentle people were first discovered living and working with great, bear-like, black dogs. In fact, all the evidence points to the Beothuck Indian Dog being relatively small, although he was probably black or grey. This particular tribe does not appear to have used its dogs a great deal for draught purposes, although they were probably valued as hunting dogs. One of the earliest reports of the Beothucks describes them as being very frightened by the sight of European mastiffs.

The Vikings

Newfoundland was next settled by Viking explorers, who reached the island in about the year 1000. The Norse Sagas tell that Lief Ericson, who led the first expedition, carried with him a variety of domestic animals, including a "Large Black Bear Dog". In 1010 Thorfinn Karlsefni left Greenland with another expedition which included sixty men, five women and livestock of all kinds. Unfortunately, the Vikings did not make good settlers and they did not remain in any strength for more than a few generations, at most. It is reasonable to suppose that they left behind a few of their dogs.

After the departure of the Vikings, the whole of Newfoundland was left largely unexplored for the best part of four hundred years. Greenlanders visited the island occasionally, to collect timber, up to about 1350, but no further effort seems to have been made to settle there. If the Greenlanders carried any dogs with them on these visits, it is unlikely that they left them behind.

The van Oppen Family. On the extreme left of the picture, standing, is Mrs van Oppen Standing in the centre is Mr van Oppen. The little girl with a fringe, sitting in the front, is May van Oppen, now Mrs Roberts. The dog on the left is Ch. Queen of Surrey. The dog in the centre is Hector.

Ch. Netherwood Queen with her two sons by Ch. Black and White. The Landseer was unshown. The black dog was Ch. Netherwood Donovan. Queen was owned by Miss E. Dent.

The Europeans

Newfoundland was re-discovered by John Cabot in 1497, and he was rapidly followed by sailors and explorers eager to exploit the rich natural assets they found there. The country itself had timber and minerals, while the surrounding sea held vast numbers of seals and fish.

Early writers describe the native Indian dogs in general as being of medium to small size, similar to the Greenland Eskimo dogs and usually black or black-and-white. Frobisher described the Eskimo dogs in 1577

Some personalities at Thames Show shortly before the Second World War. Third from the left is Mrs Emerton. In the centre, with a black dog, is Mrs Mona Bennett. Second from the right is Miss Herdsman and far right Miss Reid
                                          photo Walter Guiver

and said, "They franke or keepe certaine dogs not much unlike wolves, which they yoke together as we do oxen and horses, to a sled or traile: and so carry their necessaries over the yce and snow from place to place . . . And when those dogs are not apt for the same use; or when with hunger they are constrained for lack of other victuals, they eat them, so that they are as needful for them in respect of their bigness as our oxen are for us." Later, Frobisher examined one deserted Indian encampment and took from it one dog, which he described as similar to a wolf, but for the most part black.

Another explorer, writing of the "Larger or Common Indian Dog", said it was little smaller than the Eskimo dog, with erect ears but a less tightly curled tail. The coat was rough and thick, and black or white-and-black. The dogs were on the whole lightly built and about as tall as a greyhound. Their distribution was from Alaska southwards.

The over-riding impression is given that these Eskimo-type dogs were the only kind found by early explorers to North America. By the early 1600's some European influences were being felt, for Griffon wrote in 1605 of spaniel-like dogs which he found in North Virginia.

Sailors from the Western European sea-board, from Spain to Scandinavia, were going to Newfoundland by the beginning of the 16th Century. Many would have carried dogs on board, either as ship's dogs or to use for hunting and draught purposes. So it is not difficult to guess what breeds must have combined with the native Indian dogs to produce the modern Newfoundland. Portuguese Water Dogs, large Pyrenean Shepherd's Dogs; black, Basque spaniels from Spain, Sheepdogs from France and the Lowlands, and large hunting dogs from Germany and Scandinavia, must all have found their way across the Atlantic. The large, black "Guyenne" spaniels and the black St Hubert hounds from France

Harlingen Waseeka's Black Gold, sent to Britain as a gift from the Newfoundland Club of America

Naze Troll von Schartenberg. Imported from Germany, this dog played a valuable part in the breed's Post-War revival. This photograph was taken by his owner Mr Blyth shortly after the dog was released from quarantine

may even have played an early part, although they have been extinct for many years. St Hubert hounds are very beautifully sculpted in "The Vision of St Hubert" in the Chateau d'Amboise. The adult hounds look far more like Labradors than the Bloodhounds they are meant to resemble, and a half-grown puppy in the sculpture is remarkably like a young Newfoundland. From Britain would have come Mastiffs, Sheepdogs and Spaniels, including the black, Welsh variety of the latter, which died out towards the end of the 19th century.

Two other breeds which have been suggested as Newfoundland ancestors, and which are now extinct, are the Large White Estate Dogs and the Great Rough Water Dogs. There is no strong evidence that the former ever existed as a distinct breed. They were probably a type of Pyrenean or Mastiff favoured as guards by land-owners and game-keepers.

From the few pictures which exist of the Great Rough Water Dog, he appears to have been much like a large poodle, with a long, curled tail. Goldsmith described him as being web-footed, a great swimmer much used for wild-fowling and often kept in ships because of his usefulness in retrieving.

The Collie must be considered as an early ancestor of the Newfoundland. Sheep-rearing was one of the first agricultural enterprises tried by settlers on the island, and they would certainly have carried sheep-dogs with them from Europe. These early dogs would have been considerably larger than a modern Collie, since their duties would have included guarding the flocks from predators. Bewick's description of the breed suggests a large dog. He also refers to double dew-claws, though he describes them as "A remarkable singularity", sometimes also seen in the

Cur and the Spaniel. A much later writer suggested that the Newfound-land was suitable, among other things, as a herding dog. Certainly the distribution of markings on collies implies a common ancestry, particularly with the white-and-black variety of Newfoundland.

The Portuguese Water Dog must be a candidate for inclusion in the Newfoundland background. Not only does he have webbed feet, a feature shared only with the Newfoundland, the Chesapeake Bay Retriever and the pure-bred Otter-hound, but he has a considerable resemblance, particularly about the head. Two varieties of the Portuguese Water Dog have been known as pure breeds since the 14th Century: the Long-coated (Cao d'Agua de Pelo Ondulado) and the Curly-coated (Cao d'Agua de Pelo Encaracolado). These dogs were widely used by Portuguese sailors, both as retrievers of fish or equipment lost over-board and also as messengers. With the messages attached to their necks in cylinders, they would swim considerable distances between boats. A three-cornered trade existed between St Johns, Lisbon and Bristol for over three hundred years and it seems likely that Portuguese Water Dogs must have found their way both to Britain and across the Atlantic in that time.

It is also known that Biscay fishermen carried Pyrenean Shepherd's Dogs with them, and a number stayed in Newfoundland and built settlements there, keeping their dogs with them as guards of both their homes and their flocks. These shepherd's dogs would be the fore-runners of the modern Pyrenean Mountain Dog, but they were considerably rangier than

Ch. Midway Gipsy Seaolar of Perryhow. This imported American dog is seen here with his owner Mrs Mona Bennett and a six-week old son. He was Best of Breed at Crufts in 1952 and 1953

Harlingen Taaran Taru, imported from Finland and owned by Mrs Roberts

the present-day dog. It is interesting to note that the Pyrenean has double, hind dew-claws as a dominant breed characteristic, but this is only very rarely seen in Newfoundlands, suggesting only a small amount of common blood between the two breeds.

All these breeds must have combined with the local Indian dogs and subsequently interbred to produce the dog known as the Newfoundland. A harsh climate and considerable isolation would have dictated the type of dog which emerged two hundred years later. So would the demands of the

Suleskerry Seawards Sea Billow, imported from America and owned by Miss I. Morrison

Marun Kiva, imported from Finland and owned by Miss Friend

photo Anne Roslin-Williams

settlers and fishermen, who could only afford to keep dogs which were of use to them.

Newfoundland is, of course, a very large country and the communities there remain isolated even to the present day. As a result, local variations of dog appeared. The white-and-black Newfoundlands, subsequently to become known as "Landseers", came chiefly from the main island. The black dogs seem to have been more common on the off-shore islands of Miquelon and St Pierre. In particular, St John's became known for a smaller, black dog from which later developed the modern Labrador and Flat-coat Retrievers. The Chesapeake Bay Retriever is another off-shoot from the Newfoundland and is a reminder that liver or bronze are as much genuine breed colours as the more generally accepted black and white-and-black.

The Tibetan Mastiff

In the last hundred years or so, a number of canine historians have attempted to prove that the Tibetan has featured in the development of the Newfoundland. This is a very attractive theory. The almost identical appearance of the two breeds strongly suggests a relationship. However, Tibet is a very long way from Newfoundland and it is difficult to support the idea of any direct importations. It is physically possible for mastiffs to have come from Tibet, using the same route as that used by the Asiatic nomads who reached North America long before any European explorers.

However, all available archaeological evidence shows that this did not in fact happen. Furthermore, the Tibetan Mastiff is renowned for his intractable temperament and innate aggression, while the Newfoundland is an inherently gentle dog.

It seems more logical that the mastiff known to the Romans as the Molossus was a distant relative of both breeds. These huge dogs were first identified and written about at Epirus, opposite the island of Corfu. They were described as large and robust, with heavy, wide muzzles. The ears were pricked and may well have been cropped. The dogs had heavily maned necks. Colours were generally brindled or tawny. They probably originated in Asia, and travelled to Greece with nomadic tribes. Aristotle described them as sheepdogs. Later, the Romans used them as fighting dogs and Hadrian is known to have brought them to Britain. He even appointed an officer, whose sole duty was the supervision and breeding of fighting dogs. Many of these mastiffs remained in Britain, and elsewhere in Europe, after the dissolution of the Roman Empire.

Some of the descendants of these big dogs certainly found their way to Newfoundland. Two mastiffs called Foole and Gallante were taken from Bristol by Capt. Martin Pringe in 1603, and from his journal, it is obvious that guard dogs were considered a normal part of an explorer's equipment. Foole and Gallante were trained to carry half-pikes in their mouths and Pringe wrote that the sight of these huge dogs charging with their pikes was enough to route the Indians completely. There is a copper-plate engraving in existence showing the two dogs in action.

In 1609, John Guy was chartered to carry people and all forms of domestic livestock from Bristol to Newfoundland. He continued to send fresh stock out from England for a further five years. The Merchant Venturers of Bristol traded with Newfoundland from the late 1400's

Avalon's Ikaros of Littlegrange, imported from Holland and owned by Mrs Warren

onwards for another five hundred years. It seems that this was the most likely route for mastiff blood to have reached Newfoundland, rather than from Tibet.

Early Imports to Britain

It is not known exactly when the first Newfoundland dog came to Britain. Goldsmith, in the latter half of the 18th Century wrote, "This dog is of but recent introduction to this country from the island whose name he bears, and may be considered as a distinct race." From then onwards, increasing numbers were brought into Britain and they became enormously popular. Doubtless they were considered something of a status symbol in the early years and most country houses of consequence had one at some

Lasso v.d. Weilerhoher, imported from Germany and owned by Mr K. Frost.

time in their history. It must be remembered that, for those seeking an imposing dog of good temperament, the Newfoundland had few rivals. The St Bernard, then known as the Alpine Spaniel or Alpine Mastiff, was little known outside Switzerland. The Great Dane was kept mainly as a carriage and guard dog. Mastiffs were chiefly known as game-keepers' and butchers' dogs, and were rarely kept as pets. The Newfoundland's disposition made him a good children's companion and guard. His size made him a useful substitute for a pony in the nursery. In those days of large houses and cheap labour, his bulk and the mess his paws made were probably not considered too much of a disadvantage. In addition, he was a good gun-dog.

The trade in Newfoundlands started in Poole and Bristol, later spreading to Hull, Dundee and other ports. Poole has had a very special re-

Shermead Bijou of the Thatched Roof, imported from Holland and owned by Mr and Mrs J. Adey   photo Vernon Brooke

lationship with Newfoundland for over four hundred years and its early prosperity came almost entirely from the timber trade with that country. Many ship's masters soon realised they could make a useful side-line out of bringing dogs back to Britain. Some were brought in as a result of direct commissions, many came to be sold at quay-side auctions. Others were taken to London and other cities, to be sold there.

It says much for the temperaments of these early imports that they suffered the deprivations of a long Atlantic crossing, were sold to total strangers and yet quickly earned a reputation for dignified good temper.

Col. Hawker, a well-known sporting writer, said in 1825, "Poole was, till of late years, the best place to buy Newfoundland dogs either just imported, or broken-in, but now they are become much more scarce." The captain of the cutter Mountaineer was still importing dogs in 1865.

Not only the English gentry valued the qualities of the Newfoundland. The traders of Poole soon realised they were the solution to the town's traffic problems. The narrow, winding lanes, running down to the quay-side, were not wide enough to allow horses and carts easy access, and dog-carts made a useful alternative. An historian, writing of life in the town in 1830 said, "One of the usual sights of Poole in those days was still the dog-cart. The Newfoundland dogs were considered the best dogs for this and

Poole was the centre for such dogs. One, two or three dogs were harnessed to a shallow cart of about two feet wide and a yard long, and these dogs were used for local haulage and domestic work around the narrow streets of Poole, as well as for fast relays in the delivery of fresh fish along the South Coast and even to London." In 1850, Parliament made the use of dogs in this way illegal, though a Mr. James Bugden was prosecuted and fined at Poole Guildhall for using a dog-cart in 1853.

By the middle of the 19th Century, the Newfoundland was losing his popularity as a gun-dog. The white-and-black dogs had fallen from favour even earlier. Flighting wild-fowl were able to see them too easily and shooting men developed a preference for the black variety. When Col. Hawker wrote, "For a punt or a canoe, always make choice of the *smallest* Newfoundland dog you can procure, as the smaller he is, the less water he brings into your boat after being sent out.", he was sounding the death-knell of the Newfoundland as a sporting breed. His smaller relative from St John's was about to take over. Some sportsmen continued to use the breed for crossing purposes with other varieties of gun-dog, in order to perpetuate his superlative water sense, but his major role from then on-wards was to be the family guard and pet.

Aus and Eng Ch. Wanitopa Comedy, shown winning one of her Australian CC's, with her owner Mr. J. Gibson　　　　　　　　　**photo Barkleigh Shute**

Gipsy von Heidenberg of Harraton, imported from Germany and owned by Mr K. Frost

Newfoundland

While the breed prospered in Britain, things were not going so well in its own country. In the late 1700's the Governor of the island granted permission for anyone who wanted, to take a dog out of the country. One convoy alone embarked seventy. Drained, both in quantity and quality by these heavy, continued exports to Europe, the animals which remained were often poor types and ill cared for. Dogs, turned loose and left to starve by their owners when they were not wanted for work, formed packs and became a major problem. By 1780 sheep-worrying had reached such proportions that Governor Edwards signed a statute forbidding the keeping of more than one dog per family. In spite of this, it was estimated in a Government survey of 1815 that $5,000 worth of work was done each month in St. John's alone, by Newfoundland dogs.

Seventy years after Governor Edwards' statute, the situation had not improved. Youatt wrote in 1854, "His history is disgraceful in so valuable an animal. The employment of the lower classes of St. John's, in Newfoundland, is divided between the cutting of wood, and the drawing of it and other merchandise in winter, and fishing in summer. The carts used in the winter work are drawn by these dogs, who are almost invariably urged and goaded on beyond their strength, fed only with putrid salt-fish, and an inadequate quantity even of that. A great many of them are worn out and die before the winter is over; and when the summer approaches, and the fishing season commences, many of them are quite abandoned, and, uniting with their companions, prowl about, preying on the neighbouring flocks, or absolutely starving."

To be fair, Goldsmith painted a far happier picture of teams of Newfoundlands pulling sledges considerable distances and then returning home, all without the aid of a driver. In addition to pulling loads of timber and fish about the island, Newfoundlands were also playing a part in their country's postal services, running relays across terrain which was impassable to horses. They continued to be used for the latter purpose as recently as 1941.

By 1883, Hatton and Harvey wrote, "There are few specimens of the

Am. Ch. Eaglebay Domino, owned by Mrs Clarke

world renowned Newfoundland Dog to be met with now on the island from which it derived its name. The common dogs are a wretched, mongrel race, cowardly, thievish and addicted to sheep-killing. By starvation, neglect and bad treatment the race has so degenerated that few traits of the original remain." The situation continued to deteriorate, until in 1890 only sheepdogs were allowed to be kept and nearly ninety per cent of the canine population was destroyed.

It is doubtful if the Newfoundland would exist today in the island which gave it its name, but for the efforts and dedication of a small band of people who set out to save it. In 1910, Earl Grey sent a dog called Bobs to Newfoundland and in 1913 Mr Bowring imported a dog called Kayle and a bitch called Native Girl. The latter was a litter sister to Ch. Ferrol Neptune, and also to Bagheera, which the Hon. Harold Macpherson

Am. Ch. Sonnyboy of Littlegrange, bred by Mrs Warren

photo Johnnie McMillan

imported from England. Between them, these dogs did much to revitalise the breed in its native land.

Early Breeding and Showing

Early Newfoundland breeding appears to have been unregulated and there are few records of pedigrees. The first properly organised dog show was held at Birmingham in 1860 and the schedules of this and subsequent shows do give the breeding of the exhibits. Even these records are not always accurate, since dogs changed owners quite frequently and sometimes their names were altered as well. Some names were very popular, so that there were a number of dogs being exhibited and bred from at about the same time with similar names. Kennel Club registrations started in 1875, and after that the situation improved steadily.

Newfoundland coat colours seem a strange assortment to the modern breeder. Henry Farquharson, a well-known breeder and exhibitor, wrote in 1882, "It is well-known by old owners of Newfoundlands that the more common colour of imported dogs was black-and-white, or bronze, or even grey-and-white, and four white feet. A white tip to the tail, a large white breast and frequently white on the head, were the usual markings of a dog imported from Newfoundland fifty or sixty years ago." An earlier writer referred to dogs entirely liver or brown in colour, or liver-and-white, and others wrote of black dogs with brindled markings or even black and tan. Early show dogs seem to have been a mixed collection. Indeed, Col. Hawker, writing on the subject of imported dogs, said, "Here we are a little in the dark. Every canine brute that is as big as a jackass and as hairy as a bear is denominated 'a fine Newfoundland dog'."

Aus. Ch. Wanitopa Gentle Giant,
owned by Mrs J. Gibson

photo Herald & Weekly Times, Melbourne

Ch. Friendly Drelb of Esmeduna, owned by Mr Gentile   photo Diane Pearce

Dog shows and a desire by breeders to fit their dogs to what they felt to be an ideal standard gradually resulted in greater uniformity, until black and white-and-black became the generally accepted colours. However, occasional variations have continued to occur to the present time, when both grey and bronze animals have been bred.

Reference is often made by writers of this period to black dogs with a "rusty tinge" or "rusty-dun" markings. Many felt that this brown shading indicated true native breeding and preferred it to a dense black coat. Most modern breeders would consider this colour typical of the dilution which occurs just before the start of a seasonal moult. A similar bronzing effect can be seen in black Chows, if they are allowed to lie out in strong sunlight. Nevertheless, there does seem to be a tendency for this to occur more obviously in some families than others.

At the Birmingham Show of 1860, first prize went to a bitch of Lt-Col. Ing's, exhibited in a class of six. She was described as "The handsomest ever seen, and had been bred at St. John's from the best stock in the colony."

By 1862, numbers had improved. At the Agricultural Hall, classes for both sexes were provided and the entry had risen to forty-one. Mr Minton's Nigger won a first prize and Mr Davies's two bitches both won their classes. Second prize in dogs went to Mr Van Hare's Napoleon who, as well as being a show-dog, appears to have had a distinguished stage career. His owner described him as being a most sagacious animal, requiring only one lesson in which to learn each new trick. His repertoire included playing a game at cards, performing the three-card trick, trotting to music, leaping bars, through balloons and off a spring-board over a number of horses and "Other feats of a fascinating nature."

In 1864, at the Agricultural Hall, the Prince of Wales won a first prize with his dog Cabot. Three years later, the name of the Rev. S. Atkinson first appeared in a show catalogue. He was to continue showing for some years, but his best dog was Cato, who was much used at stud. He was described as black with a white mark on his chest and said to be an exceptionally fine dog. Cato won well for some years, but his greatest moment of glory came in 1870, at Newbiggin-by-the-Sea, when he rescued a lady from drowning, as well as his master who had gone to her aid.

Numbers at shows fluctuated for some years, but a peak was reached in 1892 at Preston, when the well-known breeder Mr Mansfield judged and attracted an entry of one hundred and twenty-eight.

Other winning dogs at this time included Mr Milvain's Heenan I and his son Heenan II. Leo, an imported dog registered in 1875, was black with a rusty tinge, standing thirty inches at the shoulder and weighing one hundred and thirty-six pounds. The first champion in the breed appears to have been Mr Evans's Ch. Dick, who was black-and-white, "Black head with white blaze, perfect saddle, black rump and heavy white tail."

Another important dog was Dr Gordon Stables' Ch.Theodore Nero, from St. John's. He was completely black and stood thirty-one inches at the shoulder. He won well and his descendants were to have considerable influence on the breed. Dr Stables was one of the great "dog-men" of that time and kept a number of other breeds, as well as Newfoundlands. His writings on canine matters were full of good sense and refreshingly free from the cant which so bedevilled much contemporary work on the subject. There is a delightful photograph in existence of the doctor with his Romany caravan and horse, and surrounded by a happy, mixed collection of dogs. He frequently toured England with this caravan, accompanied by the dogs and two men-servants. One of the latter attended to the doctor's clothes and food, while the other walked ahead of the caravan with a red flag to warn on-coming traffic of their approach. Dr Stables was the first writer to use the term "Landseer" to describe the white-and-black variety of Newfoundland.

In the mid-1870's, the name of H.R.Farquharson first appeared in a show catalogue. He was to become one of the most successful and distinguished breeders of all time. His later writings show him to have been extremely critical of his fellows who were, he believed, sacrificing type, symmetry and proportion to uniformity of colour and markings. Unlike many other breeders, he did not favour any particular colour in Newfoundlands and he bred good specimens of both black and white-and-black dogs. A number of his dogs were registered as bronze. Mr Farquharson's kennel was extremely influential for some years and he constantly strengthened it with imports of fresh blood from Newfoundland.

Another significant kennel was that of Mr E. Nichols, who bought Nelson I from his breeder Mrs Cunliffe Lee and made him into a champion. Nelson did well at stud, siring among others Ch.Lady Mayoress, who during her show career was said to have beaten every other dog and bitch being shown, except her father. In the same litter as Lady Mayoress were three other outstanding dogs, Ch.Courtier, Mistress of the Robes and Lady-in-Waiting, who in turn produced the highly successful dog Ch.Hanlon.

In about 1878 Mr T. E. Mansfield started to exhibit with a black bitch called Zoe. With help from Mr Farquharson and Mr Nichols, he built up a very powerful kennel. He bought Ch.Lady Mayoress and also Ch.Gunville, Ch.Courtier and Ch.The Black Prince. At one time, he was said to have had between thirty and forty dogs in his kennel, all winners or the breeders of winners. Twenty years later, he sold his entire kennel to Mrs Dickson. He became a very well-known judge, and no doubt a greatly feared one too, for he was outspokenly critical of his fellow breeders. Many, he felt, were losing soundness and type in the quest for size. He also had little patience with breeders of white-and-black Newfoundlands. He felt their reluctance to breed back every few generations to black lines was resulting in dogs which were of poor type. He also voiced concern at the prevalence of light eyes in the breed.

Other winning kennels were owned by Mr Crossfield, Capt. Jolly, Mr Paterson, Mr Haldenby, Lady Sybil Tolemache, Mr Dickman, Mr J. J. Cooper and Mrs A. G. Ingleton. The latter owned Ch.Wolf of Badenoch, who carried all before him in the show-ring. From his photographs, he appears to have been a magnificent dog, with a beautiful head.

The Twentieth Century.

The Newfoundland entered the 20th Century in some strength. Mr J. J. Cooper was still actively supporting the breed and he had been joined by such enthusiasts as Mr van Weede, Mr Gillingham, Mr Bailey and Mr van

SA Ch.Highfoo Sea Urchin, bred by Mr Winston

Oppen. The last-named was the father of Miss May van Oppen, later Mrs Charles Roberts, who is still breeding Newfoundlands at the present time. Mr Cooper bred Ch.Lady Buller and Ch.Bowden Perfection and many other good dogs. He became a very popular judge in later years.

Other successful breeders at the beginning of this century were Mr Horsfield, Mr Fearn, Mr Sheldon and Mrs Vale Nicholas. Mrs Nicholas later married Col. Wetwan and together they continued an interest in the breed for many years. Mrs Wetwan bred Ch.Shelton Viking, sire of four champions including Ch.Gipsy Duke, and owned Ch.Donovan II and Ch.King Stuart.

A few years later Miss Goodall started breeding Newfoundlands. She built up a kennel which was virtually invincible for a long time. Although her kennel was registered under the name of Starbeck, she does not appear to have used this as an affix at all. Instead, all her dogs' names were prefixed by the word "Gipsy". Among her champions were Peeress, Princess, Duchess, Boy and Baron. The greatest of all was Ch.Gipsy Duke, who still holds the breed's record of Challenge Certificates with twenty-two. He was a beautiful, all-black dog and as successful at stud as he was in the show-ring. His most outstanding off spring was probably Ch. Zingari Chief. Sadly, Duke, who was a much-loved house-dog, was deliberately poisoned in 1914, together with another young dog. One other important dog bred by Miss Goodall was Ch.Shelton King, who in turn sired Ch.Siki.

In about 1905 Harry Keeling, later Secretary of Birmingham National Show, started a kennel which continued until the First World War. His niece Mollie Crump became familiar with the breed as a child and later owned Windley Wendy and Shelton Storm Queen in partnership with her uncle. Her particular favourite was the white-and-black dog Harlingen Cedric, which she owned for a time. Although it is some years now since Miss Crump owned a Newfoundland, she still maintains a very active interest, and she is a most popular judge of the breed.

During the First World War the breed was kept going by a small group of breeders. Very few puppies were bred and post-war recovery was slow. In 1923 only twenty-two dogs were registered. By 1928 the number had improved to seventy-five. Miss Goodall, who had worked so hard to keep the Newfoundland going through the war years, died shortly after. A few new people were coming into the breed, but with numbers of dogs so small, the genetic pool they had to use was tiny. Surprisingly, the quality remained high at this time. Mr Morgan's Ch.Black and White, Mr Bland's Ch.Seagrave Blackberry, Mr David Brand's Ch.Fisher Maid, Mrs Wetwan's Ch.Shelton King and Mr Bland's Ch.Siki were all up to standard.

Ch. Siki was destined to become all-important in Newfoundland history. Although he became a champion, he was not an outstanding dog to look at. His greatness lay in his ability to pass on good qualities to his offspring. He was widely used at stud and produced winning stock by a number of different bitches. Among others, he produced Ch.Brave Michael,

Ch.Mermaid, Ch.Gleborchd Boss, Ch.Gannel Echo, Ch.Help, Ch.Water-witch, Ch.Black Bess, Ch. Netherwood Queen, Ch.Seagrave Blackberry, Can.Ch.Shelton Cabin Boy, Can.Ch.Shelton Baron and Am.Ch.Harling-en Neptune. It was through the last three dogs that Siki's long-term signifi-cance was to become apparent.

The Newfoundland was again sadly weakened in Canada in the post-war years. He was not much stronger in America. Between 1926 and 1935 a number of British dogs went across the Atlantic, most important of which were Shelton Cabin Boy and Shelton Baron, who went to Canada, and Harlingen Neptune, who went to America. All three became champions and they had distinguished careers at stud. Shortly before the Second World War, when the breed in Britain needed new blood, a bitch, Harlingen Waseeka's Ocean Spray, directly descended from Siki, was im-

Three South African champions, Sigroc Sir Percival, Plaisance Tillicum and Plaisance Night Sentinel, all owned by Mr and Mrs Wilkins, and all British-bred

ported. After the war, she was followed by Harlingen Waseeka's Black Gold. Thus the line returned to us, strengthened with American blood, at a time when we needed it most.

No record of breed history would be complete without a reference to the Hon. Harold Macpherson. As a child in the 1880's, he knew and loved the breed, as his parents owned a Newfoundland. Later, when still only seven-teen, he tried to buy a dog for himself. His difficulties made him realise that the Newfoundland was in danger of extinction in its own country. It is largely due to his work that the breed not only survived but flourished. He started with a bitch called Guess and an outstanding dog called Jack. A dog called Bobs was sent out from England by Earl Grey at this time. He was intended for a home in the northern part of the island but was prevented from leaving St. John's by the onset of winter, so that Harold Macpherson was able to use him on his own bitch before the following spring. In this way the Westerland kennel came into being. It was a name which was to become famous throughout the world. Mr Macpherson was never inward-looking about his breeding and he made a number of imports from Europe, including the purchase of Bagheera, a litter brother to Ch.Ferrol Neptune, from Mrs Bland. Westerland Sieger earned immortality by being featured on a series of postage stamps. He has the distinction of being the only dog ever to appear on a British stamp, together with the reigning monarch's head. Int.Ch.Newton is probably the most famous show-dog from the Westerland kennel, but there have been many others. Harold Macpherson died in 1963, but his Westerland line still continues today, principally in dogs from Mrs Nutbeam's "Harbourbeam", Mrs Drury's "Dryads" and Mrs Baird's "Glenmire" kennels.

By the mid-1920's, new names were coming to join those of established breeders, among them Lt-Col. Reid-Kerr with his Gleborchd prefix and Miss May van Oppen with her Harlingen kennel. The latter, who became Mrs Charles Roberts, is happily still with us and is the greatly loved and respected President of the Newfoundland Club. Her daughter, Mrs Alice Kempster, is also qualified to judge the breed at Championship level. To have had three generations of one family so deeply involved in one breed for so long must be almost unique.

The Harlingen name is well-known throughout the Newfoundland-owning world and over many years has produced winning dogs of both the black and white-and-black varieties. Champions bred by Mrs Roberts include Am.Ch.Harlingen Jess of Waseeka, Am.Ch.Harlingen Viking of Waseeka, Am.Ch.Harlingen Neptune, Ch.Harlingen Coastguard, Ch.Harlingen Pirate, Ch.Harlingen Drifter, Ch.Harlingen Sandpiper, Ch.Harlingen Safe Harbour, Ch.Harlingen Brigantine and Ch.Harlingen Black Cherry.

In 1924, Mrs Roberts imported Judith van de Negerhut from Holland. She was bred by Mr Pieterse, one of the greatest experts in the breed. Throughout his long career in Newfoundlands, he worked hard to produce sound dogs of correct type. Above all, he bred for typical, weather-resisting coats. Sadly, Judith failed to breed for Mrs Roberts and she was passed on to Miss Deane and her mother. Other imports to the Harlingen kennel included Roland van Gunzthal, only lightly used at stud, the influential white-and-black dog Harlingen Cedric, and two bitches, Harlingen Waseeka's Ocean Spray and Harlingen Waseeka's Black Gold.

Meanwhile, Judith van de Negerhut was successfully mated to Miss Herdsman's dog Ch.Captain Courageous and produced two good dogs in Black Cloud and Peter the Great. A little later, Miss Deane acquired a dog by Ch.Siki, called Brave Michael, and showed him to his Championship. He was bred in Mr Heden-Copus' successful kennel. Michael had a good career at stud. Mated to Judith, he sired Dutch Ch.Uncle Tom Detto Maso and Am.Ch.Bulwell Aero Flame, as well as Ch.Water Rat. He also sired Ch.Midshipman, when mated to a bitch of Miss Deane's, Freya of Avalon. Miss Deane owned another good dog, Roy the Magnificent. She is still actively supporting the breed and is a good example of how loyal owners become, once they have had a Newfoundland.

Judith van de Negerhut was mated to Ch.Brave Michael in 1930 and one of the puppies in the resulting litter, Aunt Chloë, went to Mr and Mrs Vernon Handley, who already owned a dog called Duke and a bitch called Harlingen Lou. The following year they acquired Faithful Roger from Mr Heden-Copus. It was largely through Mr and Mrs Handley's efforts that the Newfoundland survived the Second World War, as they somehow managed to keep a nucleus of dogs going through that very difficult time of restrictions and rationing. Among the dogs they kept was Mrs Roberts' white-and-black bitch Harlingen Waseeka's Ocean Spray, which had been imported from America just before the war started. One litter was bred from her by Bulwell Michael and a bitch from this mating was kept and bred back to her father in 1943. This was the only war-time litter to be bred and a dog puppy, Brave Serestus, was kept by Mr and Mrs Handley. This dog appears in every one of the litters registered in the immediate post-war period, and he sired four champions, Suisseberne Sealore of Perryhow, Sea Shanty of Perryhow, Harlingen Black Cherry and Harlingen Aphrodite of Fairwater.

After the war, Mr and Mrs Handley added Patriot of Witchazel and Phaedra of Fairwater to their kennel. In 1957, a Fairwater litter by Patriot and out of Naze Snowdrop (bred by Mr Blyth) produced three champions, Achilles of Fairwater, Sparry's Amphitrite of Fairwater and the outstanding dog Achates of Fairwater. Achates sired Ch.Harlingen Sandpiper, Am.Ch.Eaglebay Domino, Ch.Bonnybay Mr Barrel and Aus & Eng.Ch. Bonnybay Jasmine, the last two from Ch.Bonnybay Nona of Sparry. In 1967, Miss Friend bred another successful Fairwater champion, Lord Hercules, who has also done very well at stud. To date, he has sired Ch. Laphroaig Attimore Aries, Ch.Attimore Aquarius and Ch.Attimore Minches, as well as a number of other winning dogs. This kennel is still producing good stock to show in the near future. Today's breeders owe Mr and Mrs Handley a great deal, not only for their loyal care for the breed through difficult times, but also for the hard work they have done for the Newfoundland Club.

Mr Bland, the owner and breeder of Ch.Siki, continued his interest in Newfoundlands until shortly before the war. He also owned Siki's two litter sisters, Kaffir Girl and Maori Girl, who distinguished themselves as broods, as well as Seagrave Belle and Ch.Seagrave Blackberry. He bred Mr Morgan's Ch.Black and White, an outstanding Landseer dog, although he lacked the correct blaze. Mr Morgan continued in the breed after the war, and in 1963 he imported two Newfoundlands from Finland, a dog called Harmonattan Okay and a bitch called Marun Kiva. They produced two champions of considerable importance, Lord Hercules of Fairwater and

Sigroc King Neptune. Mr Morgan was for a time President of the Newfoundland Club.

Miss Herdsman came to prominence a few years before the war with her lovely dog Ch.Captain Courageous, the sire of Ch.Black and White. She also owned the bitch Ch.Help. After the war, she registered the affix Witchazel and continued to breed until the late 1950's. The last champion she owned was Harlingen Black Cherry, bred by Mrs Roberts.

Two owners of very large kennels in the 1930's were Miss Topham and Mr H.S.Gunn. Miss Topham's Middleham kennels were extremely successful for a time. Her best dog was probably Ch.Sebastian of Middleham. Mr Gunn, together with his wife, owned a large number of dogs, including Ch.Water Rat, Ch.Mermaid and Ch.Lady Marion.

Other notable breeders in the inter-war years were Col Reid-Kerr (Gleborchd), Miss Reid (Daventry), Mr Steggles (Bulwell), Mrs Emerton (Cobblegate) and Mr Brand.

Post-war Imports

The Second World War virtually brought dog-breeding and showing to a stop. In 1945, the Newfoundland's position was very weak. Most of the few remaining dogs were too old to breed from and infusions of new blood were vital if the breed were to survive in Britain. Present-day breeders owe a huge debt to those dedicated enthusiasts who undertook the rescue work by importing from America and Europe. They should also remember the generosity of breeders, particularly in America, who sent dogs here, sometimes accepting little or no payment. Without exception, they sent the best they could find and the quality of today's dogs is largely the result of their help.

Mrs Mona Bennett, whose Perryhow kennels were to become highly important for the next fifteen years, imported Midway Gipsy Seaolar of

NZ Ch.Stormsail Rothorn, owned by Mr and Mrs Hooper

Perryhow in 1951. This American dog achieved his Championship and later sired Ch.Seacaptain of Perryhow and Ch.Seagipsy of Perryhow. In addition, Mrs Bennett imported a bitch The Barribals Anca of Perryhow from Holland, who appears in virtually all the pedigrees registered in the late 1950's and early 1960's. Anca produced Ch.Suisseberne Sealore of Perryhow, Ch.Seacaptain of Perryhow, Ch.Seashanty of Perryhow and Ch.Seagipsy of Perryhow.

Also in 1951, Mrs Roberts imported from America a black bitch, Harlingen Waseeka's Black Gold, and thus a wheel came full circle, for Black Gold's breeder Mrs Davieson Power had imported Ch.Siki sired stock from the Harlingen kennels almost twenty years earlier, to revitalise American blood-lines. Mrs Roberts and her daughter Alice had spent a year during the war with Mrs Power, and Black Gold was sent to England, in whelp, as a gift from the Newfoundland Club of America, to assist in the post-war recovery of the breed in Britain. Black Gold unfortunately died relatively young, when she seemed certain to win her third CC and become a champion. She left behind her three champion offspring, Harlingen Coastguard, Harlingen Pirate and Harlingen Brigantine.

In 1955, Mr David Blyth, whose knowledge of livestock breeding and genetics has been invaluable to Newfoundland breeders, imported the white-and-black dog, Naze Troll von Schartenberg, from Germany. He was to provide a valuable new line for Landseer breeders in Britain.

In 1958, Mrs Pat Handley brought in Midian Dryads Sea Anchor, bred by Mrs Kitty Drury. Unfortunately, this lovely dog had a very limited career at stud. In the same year, Mrs Roberts imported a white-and-black bitch from Finland. This was Harlingen Taaran Taru, who produced Mrs Hamilton-Gould's Ch.Harlingen Sandpiper. 1963 saw Mr Morgan's two Finnish imports and in 1967 Mrs Anne Cooper imported Dory O's Harbour Grace from America. She was handed on to Mrs Juliet Gibson, who bred Aus.Ch.Wanitopa Gentle Giant from her.

In the mid-1960's two significant imports were made. Mrs F. Warren brought the black dog Avalon's Ikaros of Littlegrange from Holland and Miss Morrison imported an American bitch, the white-and-black Suleskerry Seawards Sea Billow. Although the Dutch dog was not particularly large, he produced very high quality stock from bitches of different blood-lines, excelling in head properties and sound construction. He has sired six champions to date, Bear I Do Love You of Esmeduna, Friendly Drelb of Esmeduna, Your Sweet Bippy of Esmeduna, Greenayre Dogwatch, Attimore Royal Sovereign and Clywoods Worth Boy.

Sea Billow also distinguished herself, producing a number of offspring of outstanding soundness and water-working ability.

In 1966 Miss Davies imported the Finnish bitch Merikarhun Fay of Sigroc and campaigned her to her title. She is the dam of Ch.Sigroc Miss Me.

In recent years, a number of dogs have come into Britain, both from America and from Europe. They have not yet had time to prove themselves at stud, but they are all good quality and should produce good stock when mated with existing blood-lines. Among them are two black Newfoundlands imported from Holland and Finland by Mr and Mrs Adey, two black dogs from America imported by Mr Cassidy, and two Landseer bitches, one from America imported by Mr Blyth, and one from Germany imported by Mr Frost. Mr Frost had previously imported a Landseer dog, Lasso von der Weilerhöhe of Harraton, from Germany and this dog has produced some good puppies in the relatively short time he has been in Britain. Latest import is a Danish dog owned by Mrs Blackman.

Exports

While the British Newfoundland has been considerably influenced by importations from over-seas, the traffic has not been exclusively one-way. Many dogs have gone abroad, sometimes to climates very different from ours. That they have thrived, and often distinguished themselves in the show-ring, indicates how adaptable they can be.

Mention has already been made of the Ch.Siki-sired dogs which went to America and Canada between the wars. In addition, a black daughter of Ch.Black and White, Vesta of Waseeka, was sent out to Mrs Davieson-Power and produced three champions. She was followed by the Landseer dog Lifebuoy, the result of a father to daughter mating between Harlingen Cedric and Harlingen Anne, and the sire of Am.Ch.Waseeka's Sea Maid. A small number of Miss Reid's "Daventry" dogs travelled across the Atlantic, including the beautifully marked Landseer bitch Daventry Grace Darling, which became a Canadian champion.

After the war, three dogs went to the United States; Isambard Odin the Viking, Eaglebay Domino and Sonnyboy of Littlegrange. All gained their American titles. Friendly Drelb of Esmeduna was campaigned to his English championship by his owner Mr Gentile and then taken home to America. Harlingen Sea Shell, owned by Mr Jones, is now a Canadian champion.

The Newfoundland is becoming increasingly popular in Australia. The climate in much of the country is unsuitable for heavy-coated breeds, but in other areas the dogs adapt well. There is an active breed club and they now hold their own Championship Show each year. Australian breeders have acknowledged a considerable debt to Mrs Juliet Gibson, who went out there in the 1960's, taking her dogs with her. Two of them, Aus.Ch.Wanitopa Gentle Giant and Aus.&Eng.Ch.Bonnybay Jasmine had successful show careers and their son Wanitopa Bosun Boy is now a champion. Other significant dogs exported to Australia include Wildfields Endeavour, Captain Cook of Sparry, Kingfishereach Sea Wrack and Ragtime Drunk as a Deacon, all Australian champions, and three dogs from the Harratons kennel; Icarus, Nerine and Compass Rose.

A small number of Newfoundlands now flourish in New Zealand. Two recent imports are NZ Ch.Stormsail Rothorn and NZ Ch.Stormsail Wildthorn, both bred by Peter and Judy Oriani and owned by Mr and Mrs Hooper.

NZ Ch. Stormsail Wildthorn, owned by Mr and Mrs Hooper

South Africa is another country which does not automatically suggest itself as suitable for Newfoundlands, but nevertheless has a small and enthusiastic group of breeders. Much of their stock has British origins. Three South African champions have been sent from Britain in recent years; Highfoo Sea Urchin, owned by Mr and Mrs Buckley, and Sigroc Sir Percival and Plaisance Tillicum, owned by Mr and Mrs Wilkins. Tillicum is the dam of another champion, Pendragon Boltarson, sired by Greenayre Able Seaman.

Plaisance Night Sentinel, owned by Monsieur Engrand in France, is now an International champion.

The Newfoundland has made considerable progress in Denmark since the end of the war. Although the Danish dogs carry blood-lines from many countries, British bred stock has been very influential. Renata of Sparry, bred by Mr Gale, became a Danish champion. Storytime Cachalot, a litter brother of Ch. Storytime Whaler, had a successful career at stud, siring a Scandinavian champion and many other good quality Newfoundlands. Two bitches bred by Mrs Warren were sent to Denmark in the late 1960's; Sparry's Treasure of Littlegrange became an International champion and both she and her litter sister Black Bess have been extremely influential broods, figuring in the pedigrees of virtually all the present-day winners in Denmark.

Two dogs were sent to Holland in the 1930's, and both became Dutch champions. Monna Vanna del Serchio was by Ch.Siki, and Uncle Tom detto Maso, bred by Miss Deane, was by the Siki son Ch.Brave Michael. Much more recently, Mr Adey exported Shermead Lively Lad and subsequently brought a bitch puppy sired by him back to Britain, thus strengthening the links between our two countries.

If the absence of quarantine restrictions in Europe and other countries has meant that the influence of British dogs has been considerable, they have been even more significant in Ireland in recent years. Virtually all the Irish Newfoundlands stem from the United Kingdom. The breed is supported by a small but very loyal club, whose chairman Peter Gale has owned the successful Rathpeacon kennel for many years. Mr Gale owned an outstanding dog, Ir.Ch.Rathpeacon Achilles of Fairwater in the late 1950's, followed by Achilles' son, Ir.Ch.Rathpeacon Micmac, which won certificates at eight successive shows. Sadly, Irish breeders face many difficulties at the present time, and it would be good to think that at least some of their problems might be solved, to enable them to compete more often, both sides of the Irish Sea.

The Post-War Years

Mrs Mona Bennett did much to support the breed in the difficult years of the 1950's. She first became interested in the Newfoundland in 1924 and bought her first puppy, Gleborchd Bonny Lady, from Col Reid-Kerr in 1929. Her next purchase was Heave-Ho, which won well for her. After the war, she had considerable success with a white-and-black bitch, Fairwater Aurora. Her two imports from Holland and America were extremely valuable to the breed, which was going through a testing time of post-war recovery, and she bred a number of champions and other dogs which did well at stud, and whose influence is still felt at the present time. Many current winning lines stem from Perry how stock, not least Mr Cassidy's Littlecreek kennel, which has so far bred four champions.

Other influential breeders of the immediate post-war years include Mrs Mason (Suisseberne), Mrs Shapland (Verduron), Mr and Mrs Lucas (Bonnybay), Mr and Mrs Aberdeen (Sparry) and Mrs Henry (Storytime).

New names have since joined the post-war stalwarts and they continue to produce quality Newfoundlands. Among them, Mrs Juliet Gibson has bred four Wanitopa champions, including a true "International" in the white-and-black Wanitopa Comedy, a bitch who won titles in Australia, and England. Comedy was also campaigned successfully in the United States.

Mrs Warren's Littlegrange kennels have been consistently successful. Her first brood bitch, Miranda of Verduron, produced three champions in one litter; Cherry, Faithful and Black Jet, a rare achievement. Mrs Warren has also bred an American champion in Sonnyboy of Littlegrange. As the owner of the imported Dutch dog Avalon's Ikaros of Littlegrange, she has made a notable contribution to the breed in the last ten years.

Miss Davies, Secretary of the Newfoundland Club and owner of the

Sigroc kennels, has also done much to further the interests of the New-foundland. Her first champion was Faithful of Littlegrange, followed by Sigroc King Neptune, bred by Miss Friend from Finnish stock and so far the sire of five champions, including one International Champion. Her Finnish bitch Merikarhun Fay of Sigroc has gained her championship.

Mr and Mrs Whittaker's Esmeduna kennels have had considerable success. Their first champion was Storytime Black Pearl of Esmeduna, bred by Mrs Henry. Pearl produced Ch.I'm Dimpy Too and Ch.Pied in Crime, as well as a number of other winning dogs and bitches. To date six other champions have been bred in the Esmeduna kennels.

Mrs Denham's Attimore dogs came to prominence in the late 1960's, chiefly through the influence of an outstanding brood bitch, Wanitopa Mermaid, dam of three champions and grand-dam of three others.

Miss Morrison, who does not show her dogs, has nevertheless developed a highly successful line with her Suleskerry dogs. Three good males have come from her kennel, Sparry's Suleskerry Nightwatchman, Suleskerry Sailmaker of Fairwater and Suleskerry Steersman. The latter is the sire of one Australian, one American, one International, one Danish and two English champions. Four of these were black, although Miss Morrison's great love and interest is the white-and-black Newfoundland. She is part-icularly concerned to preserve the working abilities of the breed.

There are many others who are working hard at the present time to maintain Newfoundland quality and temperament. Theirs is an uphill struggle, with costs rising steadily and a consequent diminution in demand for puppies. However, as long as the breed remains as it is at present, in the hands of small, private kennels, able to give time and individual care to their dogs, it should prosper. They are supported by a breed club which is both active and friendly, and yet small enough to retain a personal contact with all its members. Long may it remain so.

Water Spaniel by Thomas Bewick

Ch. Wolf of Badenoch, owned by Mrs Ingleton **photo Fall**

Ch. Gipsy Princess, owned by Miss Goodall **photo Fall**

Ch. Prince of Norfolk, owned by Capt. Bailey **photo Salmon**

Ch. Lady Buller, owned by Mrs Critchley   **photo Hedges**

Ch. Shelton Viking, owned by Mrs Wetwan   **photo Fall**

Ch. Gipsy Duke, owned by Miss Goodall. This dog's tally of 22 Challenge Certificates still stands as the breed record

Ch. Zingari Chief, owned by Miss Goodall   **photo Sport and General**

Ch. Shelton King, owned by Lt-Col. Wetwan   photo Fall

Norwich Captain, a nicely-marked Landseer of the 1920's

CHAPTER TWO

The Standard, together with some explanatory notes by Mrs Claudia Handley

"Breeding does not depend solely on Knowledge, but also on an intuition for what is (1) Necessary, (2) Possible, and (3) Most Important."

Johan Pieterse

O ne of the purposes of the founders of The Newfoundland Club was "to establish the standard and type for the breed". There is no written record of a standard being formulated and distributed to members, but one can presume there was such a one for the blacks as there is a record that in November 1906 a description of the markings of the white and black variety (Landseers) was drawn up and points added to the existing scale. Two years later it was decided to reconsider the scale of points regulating the weights of Newfoundlands, but again there is no written evidence of the decisions made. It was in 1909 that the Kennel Club was asked to adopt a standard definition of type, together with a scale of points for each recognised breed of dog on their register. So it seems that until that year breed standards were not given universal recognition. In fact the Kennel Club do not include a scale of points in their present day breed standards. The standard and type adopted by our founder members was acknowledged by Newfoundland Clubs throughout the World and though there are now slight variations relating to colour it is still the basis for all Newfoundland standards.

Records do not indicate any further changes in standard until 1974, when it was amended to permit black and brown as the only solid colours and white with black markings only for Landseers.

The Newfoundland Standard

Symmetry and General Appearance. The dog should impress the eye with strength and great activity. He should move freely on his legs with the body swung loosely between them, so that a slight roll in gait should not be objectionable; but at the same time, a weak or hollow back, slackness of the loins or cow-hocks, should be a decided fault.

Head. This should be broad and massive, the occipital bone well developed, there should be no decided stop, and the muzzle should be short, clean-cut and rather square in shape, and covered with short fine hair.

Eyes. Should be small, of a dark brown colour, rather deeply set, but not showing any haw, and they should be rather widely apart.

Ears. Should be small, set well back, square with the skull, lie close to the head and be covered with short hair and have no fringe.

Mouth. Should be soft and well-covered by lips, should be neither over-shot nor undershot but the teeth should be level or scissor bite.

Coat. Should be flat and dense, of a coarsish texture and oily nature, and capable of resisting water. If brushed the wrong way it should fall back into its place naturally.

Body. Should be well ribbed up with a broad back, a neck strong, well set on to shoulders and back, with strong muscular loins.

Fore-legs. Should be perfectly straight, well-covered with muscle, elbows in but well let down, and feathered all down.

Hind-quarters and legs. Should be very strong; the legs should have great freedom of action, and a little feather. Slackness of loins and cow-hocks are a great defect. Dew-claws are objectionable and should be removed.

Chest. Should be deep and fairly broad, and well-covered with hair, but not to such an extent as to form a frill.

Bone. Massive throughout, but not to give a heavy, inactive appearance.

Feet. Should be large and well-shaped. Splayed or turned out feet are ob-jectionable.

Tail. Should be of moderate length, reaching down a little below the hocks, it should be of fair thickness and well-covered with hair, but not to form a flag. When the dog is standing still and not excited, it should hang downwards with a slight curve at the end; but when the dog is in motion it should be carried a trifle up, and when he is excited straight out with a curve at the end. Tails with a kink in them or curled over the back are very objectionable.

Male animals should have two apparently normal testicles fully des-cended into the scrotum.

Colour. Dull jet black. A slight tinge of bronze or splash of white on chest and toes is acceptable. Black dogs having only white toes and white chest and white tip of tail should be exhibited in classes provided for black. Brown can be chocolate or bronze. Should in all other respects follow the black, except in colour. Splash of white on chest and toes is acceptable. Brown dogs to be exhibited in classes provided for blacks.

White with black markings only — Landseers. For preference black head with narrow blaze, even marked saddle and black rump extending onto tail. Beauty in markings to be taken greatly into consideration. Ticking is not desirable.

The above are the only permitted colours.

Height and Weight. Size and weight are very desirable so long as symmetry is maintained. A fair average height at the shoulder is 28″ for a dog and 26″ for a bitch, and a fair average weight is respectively: —

Dogs .... 140 — 150lbs

Bitches .... 110 — 120 lbs

The measure of any true-to-type Newfoundland is all-round soundness, a soundness which embraces over-all appearance, bone structure, movement, body line, condition, size and temperament. I rate the latter quality highly in any successful development of the breed, since nobility and fortitude are as essential in true breeding as the presence of physical characteristics. Of late years it has been rare to meet with complete harmony of physical and mental attainment; size, flexibility and good temper are the basic criteria in evaluating any fine Newfoundland.

The Standard as laid down encompasses the following essentials: The dog should be strong, active, heavily built but able to move freely with, preferably, a slightly rolling gait. Weaknesses would include a hollow back, cow-hocks, overweight and sluggishness of movement.

A broad and massive head is desirable, but this without a corresponding body substance, deep-chested line and freedom of movement, is insufficient,

A dog with yellow or very light eyes should not be used for breeding, as these physical traits are against the true type. In bronze dogs, a paler, amber-coloured eye is acceptable.

As the Newfoundland must be considered fundamentally as a working water-dog, a correct coat is important. The top-coat should be straight and harsh. The undercoat, which is essential, should be soft and dense. It performs the same function as a duck's down and in a correct coat will ensure that the dog's skin remains warm and perfectly dry, even after long periods in water.

A Newfoundland must always stand four-square, on straight, well-boned legs, The front legs should be more heavily feathered than the back ones, but never to the extent of impeding the dog in snow or water. The hind limbs should push the dog along with a powerful, easy action. The hocks should be neither straight nor over angulated, as either construction predisposes to unsoundness. While heavy bone is desirable, the dog should never present a clumsy, cloddy appearance.

The ears should be small and well set back, and the tail should reach to just below the hocks.

The feet must be strong and well-rounded. The toes should be joined by a thick, flexible membrane or webbing, which is a particular feature of the Newfoundland and helps him to swim well.

DULL jet black is the perfect colour, but we have many shiny dogs these days. For the beautiful Landseer, we need a narrow white blaze on the black head, a saddle and a black rump extending on to the tail. Otherwise, the more white the dog has the better. The white parts should be pure and not marked with black ticking.

C.H.

41

iki, owned by Mr G. Bland

Ch. Brave Michael, owned by Miss Deane   photo F

Ch. Gleborchd Boss, owned by Lt-Col Reid-Kerr   **photo Sport and General**

Ch. Mermaid, owned by Mr Gunn   **photo Fall**

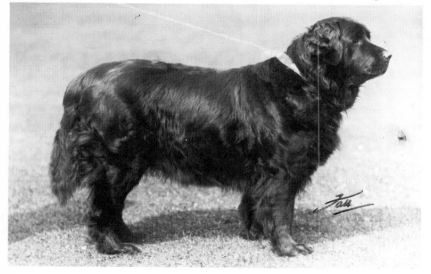

Victorian children's scrap-book cut-outs

CHAPTER THREE

Why do you want a Newfoundland?

"Sa Fierté, sa Beauté, sa Jeunesse agréable
Le fit cherir de Vous, et il est redoutable
A Vos fiers ennemis par sa courage.'

Taken from "Anecdotes of Dogs" by Edward Jesse

Anyone who has owned one of these lovely dogs will be very reluctant to change to another breed, yet he may find it hard to explain his devotion to an animal which is large and hairy and weighs something in excess of one hundred pounds.

The greatest attraction of the Newfoundland is his temperament. As a family dog he is supreme. He combines a mild guarding instinct with a gentleness which makes him a perfect companion for all generations. In particular, he has a great affinity with children. Mrs Roberts recalls losing her little girl Alice, and calling in the police. The baby was eventually found, fast asleep in a shed at the bottom of the garden, and guarded by Wendley Gipsy Queen, who gently but firmly refused to allow anyone but her owner to touch the child.

The Newfoundland is not quarrelsome or easily provoked by other dogs. This is not to say that he is a paragon from the moment of his birth. A Newfoundland puppy is just like any other, and needs firm, kindly training to make him a welcome addition to a human family. However, his natural eagerness to please makes him an easy dog to train. He has little of the desire to please himself which makes some of the "hard" breeds a challenge. He is normally robust and veterinary attention is seldom needed.

Combined with these characteristics is the Newfoundland's physical beauty. A soundly-constructed dog, well-groomed and in healthy con-

42

Newfoundlands are not quarrelsome

This is not to say . .

. . he is a paragon from the moment of his birth

dition, is a sight to gladden the heart of the least enthusiastic dog-lover. In spite of his considerable bulk, he can move with dignity and grace. His thick, slightly glossy coat, with its modest amount of feathering, adds a touch of glamour without disguising that he is essentially a working dog. The head is truly noble, but with a kindly expression in the deep-set eyes. A dog like this is a companion of whom you can be very proud, whether he walks placidly beside a baby's pram or romps across open fields.

However, before you rush out to buy a puppy, there are questions to be asked, and honestly answered.

Will a large breed of dog fit into your household, your budget and your way of life? The cuddly, eight-week old teddy-bear you bring home will be more like a leggy shetland pony by the time he is eight months old. Because he is large and not always neat in his movements, when he wants to play like any other normal young creature, he will disrupt your home more than a smaller dog. No Newfoundland will ever deliberately hurt a child, but his sheer size can make him a hazzard to very small children, who are easily knocked over.

Are you prepared to accept the extra work a large and hairy dog will make? Muddy paw-marks are inevitable. Bring a Newfoundland home from a walk in the rain and the effects of a good shake can be devastating to the house-proud. The dog requires regular grooming. A quick rub over with a hound-glove may be suitable for a short-haired dog, but more is needed to keep a dog of this breed clean and tangle-free.

Can you cope with the expense of rearing and keeping such a large dog? During the growth period, feeding costs can be very high. Even maintenance of a full-grown dog will make a substantial addition to the housekeeping bills. Dismiss any ideas you may have about recouping these costs in puppy sales or stud-fees. It is very rare for a bitch of one of the large breeds to pay for herself in puppies. It is also unlikely that a dog will support himself in stud-fees. Firstly, he will have to make a name for himself as a successful show-dog. Secondly, he will have to prove himself a good producer of quality puppies. Even then, in a numerically small breed such as the Newfoundland, he will only have a limited number of bitches brought to him.

Forget any ideas you may have had about feeding your dog "on the cheap". He needs a good, well-balanced diet. Substituting cheap cereals for fresh meat will only result in skin and digestive troubles. This is not to say that a dog needs to be fed on prime steak, but even offals and meat unfit for human consumption are costly these days. The Common Market Regulations governing abattoirs will probably make offal even more difficult and expensive to obtain in future.

When you take your annual holiday, can you take your dog with you, or can you afford to kennel him? Newfoundlands are traditionally sea-going dogs, but hot, sandy beaches are not ideal for them. Nor is it kind to subject them to long hours, shut in cars while their owners sight-see or go shopping.

44

What sort of garden do you have? Small, immaculate gardens and big, heavy dogs do not go well together.

Have you time to exercise a dog? Newfoundlands are not compulsive exercise-takers but an adult dog should have a moderate amount to keep him healthy and mentally alert.

Finally, are you prepared to allow the dog to become a full member of your family? Some breeds have independant characters. Others are perfectly happy in a kennel atmosphere with others of their kind. Not so the Newfoundland. He needs to be with his people. The cruelest thing you can do to him is ignore him. If you are going to have to exclude him from many of your family activities, it is better not to own one of this breed at all. Above all, he needs your love. He will give you all he has to offer. He deserves a lot in return.

The cuddly teddy-bear

Ch. Gannel Echo, owned by Mrs Cardell　　　　　　　　**photo Fall**

Ch. Captain Courageous, with his owner Miss Herdsman and Miss Deane's Judith v. d Negerhut

Ch. Black and White, owned by Mr Morgan

CHAPTER FOUR

Buying a puppy

"A good whelp will not come of a bad dog."

Hebrew proverb

Having decided you really want a puppy, how do you set about buying him? If you do not already know a reputable breeder, there are two possibilities. One is to contact the Secretary of the Newfoundland Club, who generally knows of available litters. She will appreciate a stamped, addressed envelope. Alternatively, go to a dog show and enquire among the exhibitors. The Secretary's address and a list of the show societies which schedule the breed are given in the Appendix. At a show, make your enquiries after the judging is over, when the exhibitors are not involved in preparing their dogs for the ring.

While the Newfoundland Club cannot guarantee puppies bought from members, it may be said that virtually all the reputable breeders in this country belong to the club and support its aims. Nevertheless, keep your wits about you, when you go to see a litter. Most dog breeders are optimists and cannot be blamed for thinking their particular goslings are bound to turn into swans. If you have never bought a puppy before, try to take a more knowledgeable friend along with you. Even then, remember that the most promising 8-week old puppy can grow into a very plain adult. The reverse can happen too, but it is less likely.

Before going to choose a puppy, enquire about its parents. You have a better chance of acquiring a sound, typical specimen if it comes from stock with a proven show record. This is not to say that a pedigree studded with champions is a guarantee of perfection, but it does indicate that the breeder is on the right lines.

If you have been to one or two shows, you may have had a chance to handle the sire or perhaps some of his off-spring. Satisfy yourself that they are sound and that they have the correct temperament. You will be able to see the mother when you go to look at the puppies. She should be healthy and friendly and free of any skin trouble, but she may be forgiven if she seems a little protective towards her babies.

When you go to view the litter, take a good look at the kennel. If it is dirty and ill-kept, the puppies will probably be the same. Use your intelligence about this. A muddy run can be unavoidable in wet weather, but piles of excrement, foul bedding, dirty dishes and stale food are another matter. Choose a puppy which is bright and friendly in appearance. Unless you are experienced and really know what to look for, avoid the pushy, "boss puppy" as well as the pathetic waif who sits in the corner. The former may turn out to be a bully and the latter may be nervous or ailing. Assuming you have already decided whether you want a dog or a bitch, ask the breeder to remove all the puppies of whichever sex you do not want. This should leave you with a manageable group to choose from.

The puppy you select should present a sturdy, compact appearance. Avoid a puppy with light bone, crooked limbs or feet which look flat or splayed. These are faults which will never come right with maturity. The front legs should be joined to a reasonably broad chest and not appear to "Come out of the same hole", but bear in mind that a puppy with an excessively wide chest frequently grows into a coarse, heavy-topped animal.

The skull should be reasonably wide between the ears, and the muzzle broad. A narrow, pointed muzzle will not broaden substantially with age. The ears should not be over-long and spaniel-like, although they will be proportionately larger than in an adult. Avoid a puppy with very small ears. They tend to go with a too small head. There should be no haw, or inner lining of the lower eye-lid, showing, though sometimes a very sleepy puppy will show haw, which disappears as soon as he wakes up.

The teeth should meet in a scissor bite (with the top teeth closing tightly over the lower ones) or in a pincer bite (with the front teeth meeting edge-to-edge). It is worth noting that the upper and lower canine jaws develop at a slightly different rate. The lower mandible frequently grows a fraction more than the upper one. This means that a jaw which, in a puppy, is under-shot (with the lower front teeth closing in front of the upper ones) is likely to be even more under-shot in an adult dog. On the other hand, a jaw which is slightly over-shot in a puppy has a gambler's chance of developing into a reasonable scissor bite. Never count on this happening if you are buying a puppy for show purposes.

The puppy's general condition should be bright, with eyes and nose free of any kind of discharge. The ears should be clean and not smell of anything but puppy. The coat of a young puppy has a dusty appearance, but it should feel soft and the underlying skin should be supple and a little loose. Any bare patches or scabs should be viewed with suspicion. The puppy should be plump, but not over-fat. A distended, pot-belly almost certainly indicates worms or some kind of digestive trouble. The puppy's breath should smell slightly of sour milk, but it should not have a strong, offensive odour.

Take your time when choosing a puppy. While it is perfectly reasonable to examine any that catch your eye, remember they are very precious to the breeder, and handle them with gentleness and tact. It is not necessary to wrench the mouth open to check the conformation of the teeth. This can be done by running the finger gently inside the lips and feeling the teeth. Ask the breeder to remove any puppy you particularly want to examine from its fellows, so that you can look him over without distractions. If you must lift the animal up, do so with great care, supporting his weight with a hand under the hind-quarters. Never lift a puppy up by the scruff of his neck or by grasping his shoulders. His joints are very loose at this stage and serious damage can result.

If you have any ambition, however modest, to show or breed from your dog, make sure you buy a puppy which is not only sound but which has the correct markings for its colour. Black, or any other self-coloured dogs, should have only a mimimum of white and preferably none at all. It must be confined to the chest, tip of the tail and the toes. The markings for the Landseer variety are clearly laid down in the Standard. While it is rare to find a perfectly marked white-and-black dog, aim as near the ideal as you can. A dog which is nearly all-white or too heavily marked with black is not very attractive. In particular, a white blaze on the head is desirable, to give the typical, Landseer appearance.

When your puppy is ready to go home with you, make sure you have made the necessary advance preparations for him. You should have found out what he has been fed on, so that you can continue with the same diet, at least for a few days, until he has settled down with you. See that his bed is ready for him, so that he can learn right from the start where his special place is. He does not need anything elaborate and it is a mistake to buy an expensive basket and bedding for him. He will grow out of it, if he does not chew it up first. A large grocery carton, with a flap cut out of one side, so that he can climb in and out easily, is ideal. Line the bottom with an old piece of blanket or towel. He will soon demolish it, but it costs nothing to replace. If he swallows any bits in the process, they are unlikely to damage his inside. Place a thick layer of newspapers under and around the box, which must be in a warm, draught-free place.

Although young puppies will always drink milk in preference to water, a clean supply of the latter should be available from the start. Water fascinates little Newfoundlands, so avoid a container which can be broken, chewed or tipped up easily.

You will probably take your puppy home by car. If possible, take a friend with you, either to drive or to cuddle the puppy. He will probably suffer a little from motion sickness, or at any rate dribble a bit, so take one or two old towels with you. The breeder may give the dog a mild sedative tablet, if you are going on a long journey. Cuddle him and reassure him. After all, he is very young and has suddenly lost all the things with which he has become familiar in his short life. If he feels warm and secure on a lap, the journey will seem less upsetting. Take a collar and lead for him. These should be the lightest and cheapest you can buy, as he will soon either out-grow them or chew them up. It is wise to take them, just in case you have to stop to allow him to stretch his legs. He will not know how to walk on a lead, but at least he will not run under the wheels of a passing car.

Before you leave for home, make sure you know what inoculations the puppy has had. This is very important, as your vet will need this information if he is to complete the pup's immunisation programme.

If you are proposing to enter any kind of breeding terms with the breeder, or a joint ownership, it is well worth using the Kennel Club's forms for registering the conditions of the agreement. This will cost you about £1 and can save a great deal of argument later on. Verbal agreements can so easily be forgotten or misunderstood ,even by old friends.

It is a sensible precaution to ask your vet to see the puppy as soon as possible after you bring him home, just to make sure that he is in good condition. The journey and change of surroundings may well cause a minor tummy upset, which can easily be treated, and in any case the vet will want to talk to you about the timing of the puppy's immunisations. If you already own another dog, see that his inoculations have been brought up-to-date well before the puppy comes home.

Puppies react differently to the disturbances of going to a new home. One thing which can be guaranteed is that the child will cry in the night for his mother. Assuming that you do not want the dog to share your bedroom (and possibly your bed), this is the moment when you must harden your heart. Weaken at this stage and it will be much harder for both of you.

Choose a puppy which is bright and friendly

There are, of course, things which you can do to minimise the agony. A small puppy is very like a tiny human baby and responds to a calm and regular routine. Do not put him to bed in an over-excited and exhausted state, with the mistaken idea that he will sleep better if he is tired-out. He will behave just like any other over-wound child.

He should have been taken (not put — there is a difference) into the garden and allowed plenty of time to relieve himself. When he has performed praise him gently and then pop him into bed. Tell him to STAY. He will not understand what you are telling him to do, but it is never too early to start repeating a few basic commands. Turn out the light and shut the door. Resolve not to open it until the morning. Try to make sure that the house-hold is quiet, so that he does not hear things going on without him. If this routine is followed each night at the same time, he should adjust to it within a week or so.

Some puppies can be comforted by having an old-fashioned stone hot-water bottle, not too hot and well-wrapped in a piece of thick cloth, placed in the bed with them. Sometimes a Bonio or a large, raw (never cooked) marrow-bone will take the little sufferer's mind off his loneliness. Some owners have found that a loudly ticking clock comforts puppies. There is a theory that the ticking acts as a substitute for the mother's heart-beats. Whatever you do will probably not have much effect, beyond easing your own mind a little.

It is unreasonable to expect a young creature to last through the night without relieving himself. So be sensible about how you position his bed and put him somewhere where he cannot spoil an expensive floor-covering. The area around his bed should be covered in newspaper. Never scold him for making messes on the papers. During the day, take the puppy outside at regular intervals, especially after waking or after a meal. Always go to the same spot, as the smell will help to trigger-off the required response. Whenever he spends a penny, praise him as lavishly as your sense of the ridiculous will allow. Your neighbours may think you mad, but the puppy will soon learn what is required of him, if you are patient and ultra-vigilant at this early stage. Never shut him outside on his own during these early days. All he will do is work himself into a state, screaming to be let in.

Some people find that a puppy becomes trained quite quickly and easily if the newspapers are gradually moved closer to the back door, and then finally taken outside. Once the dog has learned to ask to be let out to perform on the papers, they can be dispensed with altogether.

Newfoundland puppies are not hard to house-train, though dogs may be a little slower on the up-take than bitches. It is vital to praise when the puppy does the right thing and not to frighten him with harsh scolding when he errs. It is not necessary to rub the dog's nose in his mess. He will not even remember how it came to be there. You have a major responsibility to help. He cannot hope to control his immature muscles any more than a human baby can, so never expect too much of him.

With general training, use your common sense. Never leave temptation in a puppy's way. Never place him in a situation where he can damage your property. Shutting him up in the living-room, because you cannot cope with him under your feet in the kitchen, will simply result in chewed furnishings. Be sensible about giving him toys. He desperately needs to chew at this age, both to help his emerging teeth to come through and also to occupy himself. Give him something appropriate to work on. If you give him an old slipper or an abandoned child's toy, do not be surprised if he then regards all slippers and toys in the house as his. How on earth is he to know the difference? Teach him gently that hands are not for biting. What is an amusing game when he is tiny can be very painful when his teeth are larger and his jaws stronger, but he will not know the difference. Do not encourage him to jump up. For one thing, it can damage his hip joints, which are very loose and soft at this age. For another, if he continues the trick when he is a few months older, it can be both annoying and danger-ous. A knee pushed firmly into his chest, supported by the command NO! will soon teach him not to jump up. Always praise him when he does right and scold him gently when he errs, and when you are certain that he understands what he has done wrong. You must catch him in the act. Five minutes later, he will have forgotten what it was that he did. Newfound-lands are very sensitive to voice changes and their natural eagerness to please those they love makes them easy to train. Smacking should never be necessary, if you have laid the correct foundations right from the start.

Housing

The Newfoundland has been designed by nature to withstand extremely harsh weather conditions. This means that, in Britain's moderate temp-erature, he is perfectly happy living out-doors, provided he has a dry, draught-proof shelter in which to sleep. This also means that he does not fit in comfortably with the over-heated type of housing which many people now take for granted. However, the Newfoundland is also an extremely sociable animal, who cannot fulfil his potential as a family companion if he is shut away from his human friends for long periods.

So some kind of compromise is necessary. The dog will be happy spending most of each day out in the garden, particularly if he can find a vantage-point from which he can watch some human activity. Some quiet corner of your kitchen will suit him very well at night. He requires no elab-orate bed or bedding, provided he is not lying in a draught. However, it must be HIS corner, where he is out of range of passing feet and where he has sufficient room to stretch out completely.

If you decide that the dog must be housed outside, then it is kind to see that he has another dog for company. His sleeping-place does not need to be very grand, but it must be draught-free, large enough for him and with the floor raised at least 3″ above the surrounding ground. It should be positioned so that it is sheltered from wind and strong sun. Place it where he can see and hear family comings and goings. If you are housing the dog in a purpose-built kennel, make sure that the roof is sound and that water drains off it efficiently. Corrugated-iron roofs have very poor insulating qualities. The kennel should be well-ventilated. The opening for the dog need not be very large, but make sure that there is a reasonably large door for you to use. You will find cleaning a miserable chore if you have to struggle in and out of a small entrance. If you intend using the kennel for breeding, it needs to be large, not less than 8′ square. Ideally, you should also have electricity laid on. If you have to attend to a whelping bitch in the night, you will need a decent light, and also a means of heating the kennel.

If you intend converting an existing stable or out-building into a kennel, examine the walls for damp and if necessary, line them. They need only be lined to a height sufficient to protect the dog from leaning against damp stone-work. An enclosure of straw bales works well and the straw is useful in the garden when it needs to be changed. Alternatively, you can line the walls with either plywood panels or tongued and grooved boards. These should be attached to the masonry with wooden battens not less than $\frac{3}{4}″$ thick, so that a current of air may pass between the two layers. The walls will have to be scrubbed down with disinfectant from time to time, so that porous materials like hard-board are not suitable liners.

The dog must not be allowed to sleep on a damp floor, so provide him with some kind of base on which to lie. Old floor boards, or a chip-board panel, laid across a few rows of bricks or old wooden joists work well. It is not unknown for Newfoundlands to shun the most perfect of beds and prefer a cold, concrete floor, If they do, they will be vulnerable to both rheumatism and pressure sores, so try to encourage your dog to sleep in the correct place.

Bedding need not be expensive. A large piece of old carpet will do. It is worth having a duplicate piece to use when the other is being cleaned and aired. Straw is satisfactory and the dogs love nestling into it, but it has the disadvantage of harbouring parasites. The danger of this is less if you use old straw, at least a year after harvesting. Hay is not suitable, particularly for young puppies. It contains sharp stalks, which can damage eyes, and also seeds which can work their way into ears and eyes and cause inflammations.

An excellent bedding material is wood wool. It is parasite-free and smells pleasant. Large, compressed bales can be obtained from specialist suppliers. They are fairly expensive but one bale lasts a long time. A local timber merchant may be able to let you have wood wool, but it is likely to contain a mixture of woods, including some resinous ones. A friendly relationship with a near-by china shop may produce all the wood wool you need, although modern china packers are tending to use plastic packing materials. You should also check for broken china or glass in any bedding obtained from such a source. Always be careful to specify wood wool and not wood flakes. The latter break up easily and also cling to the dog's coat. Soiled bedding will have to be burned, as wood wool does not compost readily.

Three 7-week old Hambledown puppies

Old stables and outhouses are notorious for having woodwork painted in old-fashioned, lead-based paint. If this is chewed by livestock, it can be fatal, so check carefully before letting your dog use an existing building.

If you intend constructing a run for your dog, it should be made of chain-link fencing, supported by strong 4″ x 4″ posts firmly driven into the ground. A height of 4′ 6″ is sufficient to contain most Newfoundlands, although occasionally they have been known to clear up to 6′. You will need a higher fence if you want it to protect an in-season bitch from outside interference.

Unless it is very large and well-drained, a grass run will quickly become a mud run. It is also difficult to clean excreta from grass. Concrete is ideal, but not everyone can afford the considerable cost of a properly constructed concrete base. Satisfactory alternatives are a thick layer of gravel or well tamped-down cinders, but these are not suitable if you are housing a litter of puppies. Whatever you decide on, make sure that any slope is away from the sleeping quarters and from the entrance to the run, so that rainwater will not collect into puddles.

Try to site your kennel as near the house as possible. The dog will be miserable if he is banished to the bottom of the garden, and you will find it much easier to attend to his needs if he is reasonably close.

The kennel must be scrubbed down regularly with a good disinfectant. "Cromessol" is an excellent product, designed for use in kennels, and smells pleasant, The bedding should be cleaned or replaced as necessary, particularly in wet weather. Excreta must be picked-up daily.

However perfect your kennel may be, it is no substitute for the Newfoundland's proper place, which is with his people and in their home.

"Newfoundland puppies should be seen to grow like vegetable marrows."
From The Kennel Encyclopaedia by F.T.Barton

Ch. Water Rat, owned by Mr Gunn

photo Fa

Ch. Harlingen Drifter, owned by Mr Morgan

Ch. Majestic, owned by Mr Bland   **photo Fall**

Ch. Lady Marion, owned by Mr Gunn   **photo Fall**

Bulwell Michael, a well-marked, pre-war Landseer, the property of Mr Squires

Ch.Harlingen Brigantine, owned by Mrs Roberts

Harlingen Pirate, owned by Mrs Mayhew   **photo Cooke**

Ch. Suisseberne Sealore of Perryhow and Suisseberne Lifesaver, with their owner Mrs Mason   **photo Monty**

CHAPTER FIVE

The rearing and care of a Newfoundland

by

Mrs. E.M.H.DENHAM, M.R.C.V.S.

"The Newfoundland Dog is one part breed and two parts feed."

from "The Kennel Encyclopaedia by F.T.Barton

A Newfoundland puppy is usually purchased between six and eight weeks of age. It should have firm and solid feeling legs, with thick bones, and the limbs should be straight. The body should be well-covered, but not too fat. The back should not be narrow or roached, nor should the abdomen be pot-bellied. The puppy should walk firmly, without limping. It should be remembered, however, that on hot days Newfoundland puppies tend to be very lethargic, flopping around and refusing their food until the evening, when they become extremely active and eat their day's rations in one go.

Puppies can be reared on fresh food or a complete dried food. Should the latter be used, the manufacturer's instructions should be followed. It must be remembered that if they are complete foods they do not need the addition of extra vitamin supplements unless it is stated, and that sometimes irreversible damage can be done to puppies' bone structure by giving an excess of Vitamin D. This must also be remembered when feeding fresh foods. Many cereals have added Vitamin D, and an aggregate of these plus the Vitamin D which the owner puts on the food will give the pup far more than is good for it. A mixture of fresh and dry foods may also be used, but again the vitamin supplements should be cut down according to the content in the dry food.

Puppies should never be reared on tinned foods as one often has to give two or three times the weight of the tinned food to achieve the protein equivalent of fresh food, and the puppy might find it difficult to consume enough for correct growth. A good basic diet of fresh food is as follows: —

Breakfast: Cereal and about $\frac{1}{2}$ pint milk. (Porridge is the one used by the author, as it is palatable and inexpensive) A raw egg, complete with its shell, may be given on alternative days.
Lunch: Meat (ox cheek, ox neck, horse meat, rabbit, chicken or tripe) plus one-third of its volume of puppy meal, or terrier meal as the puppy grows older and wants larger pieces of biscuit. Bone flour and vitamin supplements.

Tea: Cereal and milk, as at breakfast, give about ½pint. This quantity can be increased as the puppy grows, and will take more, to one pint twice a day.

Supper: As lunch, but omitting the vitamin supplements.

Lightly cooked green vegetables and grated raw carrots may be added to the meat meal when the pup is over fourteen weeks old.

The puppy's meat ration should be as follows:

        8 — 10 weeks . . . . 12 — 16 oz per day
        10 — 12 weeks . . . . 1 — 1¼lb per day
        12 — 14 weeks . . . . 1¼ — 1¾lb per day
        14 — 16 weeks . . . . 1¾ — 2¼lb per day
        16 weeks onwards . . . . .2¼ — 3lb per day

If tripe is fed, about an extra half to a third of the quantity is necessary, as this is not such a dense meat as the other types used. The quantity of meat eaten varies enormously with the individual puppy. Newfoundland puppies are not normally greedy, so it is usually all right to give them as much as they want, unless they begin to grow too fat, when the ration should be reduced. At six weeks the meat should be minced, but by eight weeks it can be finely chopped, and at twelve weeks it can be given in larger chunks. The meat may be given either raw or cooked, but it must be properly thawed out if it has been deep-frozen.

Both puppies and adults enjoy chewing bones. Only large, raw ox bones should be given. It is dangerous to give dogs lamb, pork or poultry bones (especially chop bones) as they may splinter and damage the dog internally. Fish bones can also be harmful. Cooked bones sometimes form a cement-like mass in the dog's rectum, which causes a stoppage.

The correct dosage of bone flour is a slightly rounded dessert-spoon per lb of meat given. (Slightly less with tripe.)

The correct Calcium: Phosphorus level of dogs' food is 1.2:1, but meat has a balance varying from 1:15 to 1:50 depending on the type of meat. Liver and heart have a very high Phosphorus content. To redress this imbalance, Calcium must be added in the form of either bone flour or as Calcium Carbonate, the dose of which is a level teaspoon per lb of meat given. Calcium Lactate should not be used as far too great a quantity is necessary to redress the balance.

Various vitamins should also be added to the puppy's food. These are as follows:

Vitamin B Complex   A lack of these vitamins causes various symptoms, ranging from convulsions, anaemia, muscular weakness, to "Black Tongue" and vomiting. Black Tongue, when the tip of the tongue turns black and sloughs off, should not be confused with the splashes of blue-black pigment which many Newfoundlands have on their tongues. The B vitamins can be found in Brewer's Yeast. The dose is one 300mg tablet per 15lb weight of dog per day.

Vitamin A and D, the fat soluble vitamins. Vitamin A helps in the maintenance of healthy skin, in assisting night sight, and in bone formation, expecially of the skull. The dose is 30 International Units per lb body-weight per day.

Vitamin D is necessary for the utilisation of Calcium for building bones. A deficiency leads to rickets. Some Vitamin D is obtained from the sun's rays; it is also found in egg yolk, summer milk, and in some fish livers. As mentioned earlier, too great an excess can be dangerous as it withdraws the calcium from the shafts of the long bones in the body, and builds up in the heads of the bones. The dose is 9 International Units per lb body-weight per day. This can be increased slightly during the winter. They are given in cod liver oil; the dosage being one teaspoon per 50 lb weight of dog per day, or in Adexalin drops (Glaxo); one drop per 6lb weight of dog per day.

Instead of giving yeast and cod liver oil separately, they may be given together in various proprietory compounds, such as Vetzymes (Phillips), Canovel (Beecham), and SA 37 (Intervet), but on no account should these be given in addition. These compounds contain a certain amount of calcium but are not sufficient to balance up the Phosphorus in the meat, so a slightly reduced amount of bone flour may be given when they are used.

Milk is perfectly balanced food for the young puppy so no extra vitamins need be added until solid food is given.

The diet is maintained at the quantity given to a 16 week old puppy until it is about 15 months old. It can then be reduced a little as an adult dog does not require as much as a growing pup.

At about $4\frac{1}{2}$ months old the puppy may refuse its tea, which can be cut out and the breakfast increased, and at seven to eight months the two meat meals may be amalgamated. Fresh water should always be available to both puppies and adults. An adult dog, not in hard work, does not require such a high-protein diet, but it is very foolish to stint on food during the growth period.

When a puppy is born it weighs about $1\frac{1}{4}$lbs. From this time, to about three weeks of age it gains about $1\frac{1}{4} - 1\frac{3}{4}$lbs a week. After this it gains about 3-4lb a week until it is about six months old, when it weighs approximately half its adult weight.

If a dog or puppy becomes too fat the biscuit ration should either be cut out or substantially reduced, and the meat reduced by one-third. Greens and All-bran can be added to an adult's food to increase the bulk, if he seems hungry. A puppy is normally all right with just a reduction in quantity, as he is having milk as well.

Very old dogs sometimes benefit from having two smaller meals a day. This aids their ability to digest food.

The puppy should be wormed at six, eight and twelve weeks. This is explained in greater detail under "Roundworms".

It is important not to allow the puppy to go on slippery floors nor to stand on its hind legs for lengthy periods (eg., looking out of windows or standing in a run with its front feet on the wire), as the ligaments of the legs can be severely affected; resulting in either the front feet turning outwards at the wrist, or the back legs becoming cow-hocked, or the patella (knee-cap) becoming inwardly or outwardly displaced, resulting in the leg growing twisted. The likelihood of the puppy developing one of the above conditions is greatly increased if it has been allowed to grow too fat.

It is also a mistake to take the puppy on long walks before it is seven months old. It should be taken for short walks avoiding places where it can scramble up and down banks. The bulk of its exercise is best taken padding around its owner's garden.

Sometimes I sits and thinks . .

. . sometimes I just sits

Care of the bitch in whelp

Bitches usually come into season (on heat) for the first time between seven and nine months of age, and from then on every six to nine months for the rest of their lives. Occasionally the seasons cease when they become very old and very occasionally bitches never come into season at all. They may have a "silent heat" when the outward manifestations of the season do not occur. During these times, a bitch may conceive and produce a litter.

The season has three stages. The pre-oestrus, when the bitch's vulva swells slightly and there is a blood-stained discharge. This lasts for seven to sixteen days. The oestrus or true heat is when the vulva swells considerably and the discharge turns pink. The colour change can best be seen by wiping the bitch with a piece of cotton-wool; the colour can then easily be seen against the white background. The ova or eggs are shed during this stage, which lasts three to seven days. Towards the end the vulva shrinks and returns to its normal size and appearance. The met-oestrus is the final phase, when the internal reproductive organs return to a quiescent state. This takes about three months.

The an-oestrus follows, and during this period the ovaries are inactive, after which the cycle starts again.

The bitch must be mated during the oestral phase. One of the signs that she is ready is that when scratched above the base of the tail, she will turn it to one side. Some bitches will also do this in the pre-oestral stage and it can be difficult to ascertain when the bitch is "ready".

The bitch should not be bred from until fully matured in growth, as her development will be stunted if she has to rear puppies while still growing herself. Thus the third season, or one year and nine months to two years and three months is the earliest the bitch should be bred from. Six and a half years is the latest a bitch should be allowed to have a first litter, unless the advice of a Veterinary Surgeon is sought as to her general fitness.

It should be remembered to bring her innoculations against Canine Virus Distemper, Canine Virus Hepatitis and Leptospirosis up to date before the bitch is mated.

The duration of pregnancy is about 63 days. During this time the bitch should continue to be exercised regularly. Towards the end of the pregnancy she should only be allowed to walk as far as she wishes. The regular exercise helps to ensure that her abdominal muscles are in good tone at whelping.

The bitch should be wormed for round worms at three weeks of pregnancy and again at five weeks if any worms were seen at the first worming.

For the first four to five weeks the bitch will eat the same amount of food as normal. Then, as the puppies begin to increase in size rapidly, she should be given more meat. The quantity should vary according to the size of litter she is producing. With a large litter she may need five to six pounds of meat a day between the seventh and ninth week. Bone flour should be added, giving a slightly rounded dessert-spoon per lb of meat and a teaspoon of cod liver oil per day in the last three weeks of pregnancy.

It is a good idea to check with your veterinary surgeon as to whether the bitch is in fact pregnant, as she may have a false pregnancy. With this, she may show every sign of a true pregnancy, such as enlarging and reddening of the teats on the thirty-fifth day, and an increase in appetite and weight. If she is fed on double rations she will emerge at nine weeks with no pups and a ruined figure! The easiest time to check a bitch for pregnancy is about the twenty-eighth day. At this stage the pups are the size of golf balls and usually fairly easily palpated. After seven and a half weeks the foetal hearts can be heard with a stethoscope, but between these two times the pups may be very hard to detect.

Whelping

A whelping box should be prepared well before the date of parturition. The dimensions should be 4′6″ x 3′6″ with 9″ high sides. ie. large enough for the bitch to lie extended so that the pups can feed from all the teats easily. There should be a rail $2\frac{1}{2}''$ from the sides and $5''$ from the bottom. This avoids the pups being crushed should they crawl behind their mother, as it prevents her from lying with her back against the wall of the box. For the whelping, the floor of the box should be covered with a good layer of newspaper and an old blanket. The newspaper helps to absorb the considerable amount of fluid which is voided during the whelping and makes clearing up far easier.

It is advisable to take the bitch's temperature twice a day from the fifty-seventh day onwards. An ordinary bull-nosed thermometer may be used. Put some Vaseline on the end of the thermometer and insert into the bitch's rectum turned to one side, so that the bulb rests on the rectal wall. The normal temperature is 101.5°F but, twenty-four hours before whelping, the temperature nearly always falls to below 99°.

In the first stage of labour the bitch begins to scratch the floor or bedding, and pants and shivers. This stage lasts from half an hour to twenty-four hours, but should become progressively more pronounced. If she does not seem to be "progressing" quickly enough, a bumpy ride in a car may assist!

In the second stage of labour the bitch begins to strain. The outer foetal sac or allantois may rupture without appearing. The bitch usually rapidly licks up the fluid passed. The sac sometimes appears and hangs down from the vulva.

The mother should, of course, be able to cope with the birth of her puppies on her own, but very often she will not know what to do with the first puppy of her first litter. You should be prepared to assist her.

In the third stage of labour the puppy is born. It can either come out head first (an anterior presentation) or back legs first (a posterior presentation). It may either be born in the inner foetal sac (the amnion) or it may have ruptured this coming out. The amnion should not be deliberately ruptured when it appears as it helps to lubricate the emerging puppy. If the puppy is born in the sac, it should be freed quickly by breaking the sac and bringing out the puppy's head, or it will drown in the fluids. The pup should be held with its head hanging down, and the fluid "milked" off its face with finger and thumb, its mouth opened and the fluid cleared from between its jaws with a finger.

If the puppy is out of its sac, but still attached by its navel to the after-birth within the bitch, the afterbirth can be very gently eased out of the mother by light traction downwards and forwards, holding the cord as far inside the bitch as possible, not pulling all the time. The afterbirth can be severed two inches from the puppy's navel, cutting well below the fleshy part attached to the puppy with a pair of sterilised scissors or just tearing it off. The pup should not bleed at all from the stump, but if it does, the end can be tied off with cotton. The puppy is dried by rubbing it briskly with a warm, rough towel, and then given to the mother to lick.

The afterbirth is normally consumed by the bitch. This is quite natural and after she has eaten it, she will lick the puppy all over which stimulates it well and it will quickly find a teat to suckle if placed near them.

The bitch may become flustered if she is not left with her puppies during the remainder of the whelping, but when each puppy is coming, and the bitch is straining hard and turning round to lick at herself, it is as well to take most of the pups away temporarily. Place them in a box with a warm — not too hot — hot-water bottle covered with a blanket. This way there is less danger of accidental damage, as she may inadvertently crush one. They are then returned to her when she has finished cleaning up the latest puppy.

The length of time between the births varies from a few minutes to several hours. The last two or three pups may even be born a day later than the previous ones. It is advisable, however, to seek veterinary advice if the gap is longer than twelve hours, or if the bitch seems at all distressed.

The mother is often glad to be given drinks of milk or water during the whelping. When all the puppies are born she will settle down and look relaxed. The box can now be cleared of all the soiled paper, and new paper covered with a blanket, bedspread, carpet or felt be put down. It is important not to have the puppies on a slippery surface, as when they are suckling they should be able to push with their hind toes.

It is also important to have the room warm enough at ground level. The temperature should be maintained at 70°F for five days. If the puppies' temperature drops too low they will "fade" and die. The bitch will probably not like this temperature, but if she becomes too hot she can always be allowed away from the puppies for a while. After five days the temperature can be allowed to drop to about 65°F. If the puppies are too cold they will crawl into a big pile, and the ones on the outside of the pile will be cold and cry and try to crawl to the top of the pile, so they will be constantly moving and whimpering. If they are too hot, they will lie individually all over the box. If they are just right, they will lie together, but not piled on top of each other, and sleep well. If the puppies are kept on straw, the temperature can be a little lower, as the bedding will help to retain the puppies' heat.

After the bitch has finished whelping, her temperature may rise for three days afterwards. Anything up to 103.5°F may be normal.

It is as well to let your veterinary surgeon know when the bitch starts to whelp, but veterinary attention during the whelping is not necessary unless one of the following situations occurs: —

1. If the bitch's temperature drops to 98.8°F or below, stays there for twenty-four hours and then comes up again, it is almost certainly an indication of complete uterine inertia.

2. If, during the first stage, the bitch commences normally, shivering, panting, scratching up the bedding, etc. then stops; possibly never having had a temperature lower than 99.4°F, it also indicates an inertia. If the bitch is left, dead pups are normally born a week later.

3. If the bitch strains about three times every ten minutes and the pup is not born after two hours, it usually means the pup is coming up to the

pelvic brim and getting no further. The exception to this, is the last puppy, for which the mother may strain for several hours.

4.   If the bitch strains violently three times a minute and the pup is not born within half an hour, this indicates the puppy is probably stuck in the pelvis. The puppy may have stuck for several reasons; it may be incorrectly presented, with either its head turned backwards; one or both of its front legs going backwards; or if it is born with a posterior presentation having one or both back legs going forward, a so-called breach presentation. The puppy may be too large to be passed, or may be abnormal being a "monster" of some sort, having four back legs, two heads or hydrocephalus (water on the brain), or there may be two puppies coming together, one from each uterine horn, or a retained afterbirth can block the way of the following puppy.

It is as well to have the bitch examined by a veterinary surgeon twelve to twenty-four hours after the last puppy to make sure there are no retained afterbirths or other puppies.

Some bitches are incredibly clumsy and have to be watched literally the whole time they are with their puppies, otherwise there will be an accident and one or more will be crushed. With such bitches, it is easier to encourage them to leave their puppies between feeds after the first few days, so that they do not have to be watched continuously. Other bitches will settle down amongst the pups treading gingerly like a cat so as not to hurt them, and will move immediately a puppy squeaks.

After whelping, the bitch should be fed only on eggs and milk for two days if she has eaten the afterbirths, or she will probably have a bad attack of diarrhoea. Fresh water should always be available. After this, she should be given two meat meals (with bone flour and vitamins in the same dosage as given for puppies) and biscuit, and two milky meals a day. The amount given varies enormously with the individual bitch and with the age of the puppies, but a rough guide is her normal ration plus $\frac{1}{4}$lb meat per day for each pup she is feeding, when the pups are over seven days old. If she is not given sufficient food the puppies will not necessarily suffer, as provided there is sufficient fluid taken in, the composition of the bitch's milk will remain constant, the constituents having been drawn from her own body, which will become emaciated while the puppies thrive. The puppies take more milk as they grow older so the bitch's ration must be steadily increased. The safest way is to give her what she wants unless she appears to be growing too fat, when it should be reduced.

In the first three days after whelping, the bitch produces colostrum, or the first milk, which contains maternal antibodies which protect the puppies from various infectious diseases. These antibodies are retained in the puppies until they are approximately twelve weeks old. It is therefore most important that they should take the colostrum. It is as well to ask your veterinary surgeon's advice in having a dose of hyperimmune antiserum given to the puppies to protect them should they be deprived of the colostrum.

If there are more than eight or nine puppies, it is usually necessary to supplementary feed the extra puppies every two hours for the first week, every three hours for the second week, and every four hours for the third week. Different puppies can be artificially fed each time, so that they all have a turn at their mother's milk. There are at least two proprietary puppy milks on the market at present, "Lactol" (Shirleys) and "Welpie" (Höechst). If preferred, the following can be given:

Cow's milk . . . . $\frac{1}{2}$pt
Egg yolk . . . . $\frac{1}{2}$
Limewater . . . . $\frac{1}{2}$tsp

The mixture can be given at the dog's blood heat — 101.5°F or 38.8°C. The temperature can be gauged roughly by testing the milk on the back of one's hand. It can either be given in a baby's bottle, using a teat with a medium-sized opening, or by stomach tube, a technique easily mastered and taking only half a minute per puppy. The author prefers to use a Tiemans Bitch Catheter (43cms F.G.10 — Portex) for this, but any soft plastic tube about 3mm in diameter, with smooth ends and about twelve inches long will do. You will also need a 20cc plastic hypodermic syringe. The milk is drawn into the syringe and the catheter or tube attached to the nozzle. Milk should be squirted into the tube, so that it is not full of air. The distance from the puppy's mouth to its stomach is roughly measured on the tube by placing it alongside the pup, because it gives one confidence to know the distance in case the tube is accidentally pushed into the pup's windpipe. This is extremely difficult to do, but it does occur and on these occasions, the length of tube which can be inserted is only half the length measured from the mouth to the stomach. Moreover, the puppy would appear distressed and be unable to breath properly, so that the mistake is easily rectified. The tube is then pushed gently down over the middle of the tongue into the stomach, and the required amount of milk injected.

The approximate amounts given are the following, though these vary with the individual puppy, a larger one normally requiring more than a small one to start with.

Birth — 3 days . . . . 5 — 8ccs every 2 hours
(with 3 hour gaps at night)

3 — 7 days . . . . 8 — 15ccs every 3 hours,
gradually increasing over this time.

7 — 14 days . . . . 15 — 30ccs every 3 hours
(4 hour gaps at night)

14 — 18 days . . . . 35 — 45ccs every 3 hours
(5 hour gaps at night)

The puppies quickly become diurnal, even before their eyes open (10 — 14 days), so the night feeds can be given further apart than the day ones.

After the feed, the pup's stomach should feel full but should not bulge too much. If insufficient is being given, the pup will either to on searching for food after the feed, or will wake up too soon for its next meal.

If too much is given, either by artificial feeding, or if the bitch is feeding a small litter and has an excess of milk, the puppies will produce a green diarrhoea. This can be controlled usually by giving alternate feeds of either glucose and boiled water, a tablespoon to half a pint, or preferably "Ionalyte" (Intervet) and boiled water, one part to sixteen, and milk in a reduced quantity. When using the glucose or Ionalyte, the same quantity should be used as the milk normally given. Ionalyte is a medicine which restores the electrolyte balance of the intestine which has been disturbed by the diarrhoea, and it can normally be obtained from a veterinary surgeon. This pattern of feeding should be maintained until the motions have returned to normal. It the puppy appears weak at the same time, veterinary advice should be sought.

The snag with stomach tube feeding entirely, as in the case of orphans, is that the puppies will almost certainly suck each other, causing soreness. If this occurs they have to be separated from each other. It can be overcome by bottle feeding part of the time, say the feeds most convenient to the owner.

Weaning can start at eighteen days. There are various schools of thought whether to start meat or milk. The author has tried both and can ascertain no difference in the results. It is preferable to start with one on its own for the first two days, so that the puppy's intestine then has only one type of new food to cope with at a time.

Meat meals should consist of meat, puppy meal and bone flour, The meat must be finely minced, the excess fat having been trimmed off first, and the puppy meal should be added at the normal rate of two-thirds meat and one-third meal. The bone flour should be given at the rate of one rounded dessert-spoon per pound of meat. The food should be given lukewarm. The puppies will suck at it at first, pushing it to the far side of the dish. They can be encouraged by finger feeding for the first few days, but they soon acquire the knack of picking it up for themselves.

Milky meals should consist of cereal and milk. Well-beaten egg can also be added in the quantities already mentioned. The food should be lukewarm and the puppies encouraged to lap by covering one's fingers with the mixture and lowering them into the dish as the puppies lick them.

For the first two days about a tablespoon of the meat meal is given four times a day, before the puppies have suckled their mother. They can then "top up" from her when they have finished. More food may be given if they will eat it. The same principle is used with the milk meals, starting with two and a half ounces per pup, and allowing the mother to return to her puppies when they have finished. In this way, the bitch's milk is gradually cut down and she rarely has any trouble being "dried-off". If she has an excess of milk at five to six weeks after whelping, tablets may be obtained from your veterinary surgeon to reduce the flow.

At twenty-one days the puppies should be having the following: —

Breakfast and tea .... cereal and milk, with an egg every other day

Lunch and supper .... meat, puppy meal and bone flour

Last thing at night .... milk

They may be given as much as they can eat, but the quantities are approximately:

21 — 28 days .... $1\frac{1}{2}$ — 4oz meat per day, divided into two meals

29 — 35 days .... 4 — 6oz meat per day, divided into two meals

36 — 42 days .... 6 — 8oz meat per day, divided into two meals

Vitamin supplements at the dosage previously mentioned can be added at four and a half weeks of age, as it is inadvisable to add too many new things at once.

At the age of about eighteen days the puppies will attempt to climb out of their box and it is as well to allow them to be in a larger area from this time. The author favours having an infra-red lamp suspended from above, at the height recommended by the manufacturers (usually 30"), so that the pups have one warm area in which to lie if they wish. The floor is best covered with felt under and around the lamp, and newspapers on the rest. The puppies must not be allowed onto slippery surfaces because of their leg ligaments. Provided the weather is not too wet they can begin to go outside from four and a half weeks onwards, at first for short spells but after a few days they can have a kennel with a large run. They can either continue to have felt as bedding, or can have straw at this point. The run can be either cement or earth, but whichever is used, the puppies' motions must be removed twice daily. Clean water should always be available.

When the puppies are between six and eight weeks old, the mother will often regurgitate her food for them to eat. This is an interesting reflex, presumably dating back to the time when dogs were wild.

Barren bitches

Bitches are sometimes very hard to get in whelp. There are four reasons for this: —

1. The bitch has been mated either too early or too late. It might be possible to leave her with the owner of the stud dog the next time, so that she can be mated when they think she is ready.

2. The bitch has an infection which either prevents conception or causes an abortion. A swab can be taken by a veterinary surgeon to test for any infection, as there are several types of bacteria which can cause sterility.

3. Hormonal. It sometimes helps to give the bitch a dose of so-called Luteinising Hormone within four hours of mating, which helps the formation of the corpus luteum, which is necessary for the maintenance of

pregnancy. Another hormone, Progesterone, sometimes has to be given to maintain a pregnancy as well.
4.   No accountable reason.

Diseases associated with parturition and very young puppies
Fading puppies
   Fading usually occurs within the first three days of life, but can be seen in puppies up to three weeks old. The puppies begin to cry in a whining tone, go limp and seem to have no sense of direction. They become dehydrated (the skin on the neck stays in a ridge if pinched up) and they die, usually within a few hours. There are several causes.
1.   The room temperature is too low, or much too high.
2.   A bacterial infection. There are several of these, one of which may be the bitch having a mastitis.
3.   Canine Virus Hepatitis, which can affect very young puppies in this way.
4.   Insufficient food, either because the bitch has too little milk, or sometimes because she has too much and the mammary glands become engorged and painful, so the pups cannot suck. If there is a lack of milk the pups will pull long and frantically at the teats, go from one to another and then do not sleep properly, and wake up too early for the next meal.
5.   Congenital defect. Puppies sometimes fade due to internal congenital defects, also with paralysis of the recurrent laryngeal nerve — see under Congenital Defects.

Congenital Defects
   Puppies can have various congenital defects. Cleft palate, the usual defect of the mouth affecting new-born puppies, resulting in the pup not being able to suck properly, has never been seen by the author in Newfoundlands; but a paralysis of the recurrent laryngeal nerves is seen from time to time. A pup with this will suck strongly but the milk will come down its nose. It will then "fade" through hunger two or three days after birth. These puppies are unable to swallow properly. The condition appears to occur with varying degrees of severity, and it may be possible for a pup to swallow just sufficient to keep it alive until weaning time. Strangely, the pup can swallow solid food normally and it will gain weight rapidly once it is off a liquid diet. Some of these dogs may always have difficulty swallowing liquids, others appear perfectly normal by the time they are a few months old. A similar condition occurs in thoroughbred horses and is thought to be hereditary, so that these animals should never be bred from.
   If a puppy is born with distorted legs, it is better to have it destroyed right away. Another congenital defect occasionally met is a badly over-shot jaw. This can give trouble with the canine teeth on the lower jaw digging into, and making holes in, the dog's palate. It may be necessary to have the tips of the lower canines filed down by a veterinary surgeon. Wry jaws are also sometimes encountered. The condition may not show until the puppy is three to four months old.

Diarrhoea

The bitch may have slight diarrhoea for a few days after the birth, which can often be cured by giving kaolin and morphine mixture, two tablespoons three times a day. If the diarrhoea is bad and the bitch seems ill, veterinary advice should be sought.

Puppies often get a green diarrhoea if overfed, as previously mentioned, and it should be treated as described in the section dealing with the artificial feeding of puppies. They also suffer from a yellow, bubbly diarrhoea sometimes, and if this will not clear quickly by treatment with glucose and water, or Ionalyte and water (dosage as before), veterinary advice should be sought if the pups seem at all distressed, as antibiotics may be necessary to cure the condition. However, if too many days of antibiotics are given to puppies with diarrhoea, the intestine is sterilized completely and the pups can get a persistent diarrhoea because of the use of too much antibiotic.

Round or Hook Worms can also cause diarrhoea. In Great Britain puppies are usually infected with the former. The symptoms are dealt with under a separate heading, but puppies can be wormed from seven days of age onwards if necessary, using Piperizine Citrate. For young puppies it is easier to give drops of "Antipar" (Burroughs Wellcome) — 4 drops per 1lb weight, or 1cc per 3lb weight.

Eclampsia

This condition is due to a calcium deficiency which can develop even though a bitch is given sufficient calcium in her diet. The calcium in the bitch's milk is taken from her blood, which is replenished by calcium being withdrawn from the bitch's bones by the blood. If something goes wrong with this releasing cycle the blood calcium drops to dangerously low levels and the bitch shows signs of a calcium deficiency or eclampsia. There are two sets of symptoms.

1. The bitch shivers, pants, staggers and finally loses consciousness and dies if not given emergency veterinary treatment, in the form of an injection of Calcium Borogluconate intravenously. This results in a spectacular recovery. The condition may occur at any time during lactation.

2. If there is a chronic calcium deficiency, the bitch becomes restless, and overlicks the puppies, not allowing them to suckle for more than a few moments at a time. They then begin to cry and the mother becomes more agitated. She may shiver and pant and scratch up the bedding and the puppies begin to fade through hunger. This condition should be treated by a veterinary surgeon, who will probably sedate the bitch as well as give her calcium. If the bitch is not too bad, sometimes sedatives alone will suffice. Either barbiturates or promozine derivatives are normally used. Bromide is rarely strong enough. A bitch may have this condition for the first three days after whelping and then improve automatically, but it may persist for up to fourteen days. Sedatives should be administered until the animal is

normal. The condition can be brought on by too many people coming to see the puppies and getting the mother over-excited.

If the bitch suffers from either form of eclampsia, it is as well to start weaning the puppies as early as possible after the sixteenth day and it may be necessary to supplement the puppies' food from the onset of the illness.

Metritis or inflammation of the uterus

The bitch runs a high temperature, usually within seven days of whelping, goes off her food and passes a purulent yellow-red discharge from her vulva. Her milk dries up and she appears very ill. It is due to a bacterial infection and must receive veterinary attention at once.

Mastitis

The mammary glands grow hard and they and the teats turn purplish-red. The milk may change to a yellow-green and may dry up. The bitch runs a high temperature. The condition needs veterinary attention, but can be eased in the early stages by milking out some of the excess milk with finger and thumb.

Injuries to puppies' limbs

As mentioned earlier, it is very important to keep puppies on non-slippery surfaces, especially if the puppies are very heavy. The conditions which can develop as a result of, or are predisposed by, slippery floors are the following: —

1.   So-called "swimmers" or "splay" puppies. This is when the pup cannot get up on its legs at all and looks as though it is swimming. This condition is often exacerbated by the puppy having a bad infestation of round worms which makes it pot-bellied. The treatment is to worm the puppy and to put it onto carpet or felt so that it can grip. Splays nearly always recover within ten or fourteen days.

2.   Cow hocks developing.

3.   Luxating or displaced patella. The knee-cap or patella swings too far inwards or outwards and becomes lodged outside the groove in which it normally slides. This can cause the whole leg to grow crooked.

4.   Turning out of the front feet from the carpus or wrist, due to stretching of the ligaments around this joint.

Should any of the last three occur, the puppy must be made to lose weight by cutting down its food intake. If a puppy is too heavy, the condition almost always grows worse.

Rickets

Insufficient Vitamin D in the diet, leading to enlargement of the joints and the limbs growing crooked. The treatment is to give extra Vitamin D at double the normal dose until the condition has improved.

Juvenile osteo dystrophia

Caused by an imbalance of calcium and phosphorus, i.e. too much meat, not enough bone flour. The walls of the puppy's bones become thin and the bone grows in a distorted way and the puppy has difficulty in standing up and walking. This must be treated by a veterinary surgeon. General treatment must be to cut down on the quantity of meat given by almost half and increase the biscuit and milk.

Diseases of dogs' bones and joints

Hip dysplasia

This is a condition which adversely affects all of the large and heavy breeds of dog. There is an abnormality in the shape of the hip joint involving the femoral head and the acetabular cavity. The exact cause is not known but there are several theories. These are: —

1. Hereditary malformation of the joint.
2. An hereditary predisposition, which may be due to an inheritable high level of oestrogens (female sex hormones) present in some animals which causes loosening of the ligament attaching the head of the femur to the acetabular cavity, causing more "play" in the joint than is normal, which leads to the malformation of the joint during development.
3. Mineral or vitamin imbalance. The calcium/phosphorous ratio being wrong, which causes bone malformation and/or excessive Vitamin D intake, which withdraws calcium from the bone shafts and deposits it in the heads of the bones.
4. Injuries or over-exercising when too young, and standing on the hind legs too long when growing. This is made worse by the puppy being too fat.
5. A combination of some or all of the above.

The symptoms are usually seen first when the dog is four to nine months old. There is difficulty in standing up and the dog appears in pain. Its hind feet are very close together when walking and they sometimes actually cross over. In bad cases the dog staggers and sways as it moves .In older dogs arthritis often develops in the hip joints as a result of the dysplasia. The dog often stands with his hind feet pushed forward underneath the body, in an attempt to reduce the strain on the hip joint.

Treatment

If the condition proves too bad on X-ray examination, the puppy may have to be destroyed. However, many are successfully treated by amending the diet and reducing the weight of the puppy. Both meat and meal should be reduced.

There are two operations which are also successful. One is the removal of the head of the femur, which stops the pain caused by the two uneven surfaces rubbing on each other. The dog takes about three months to recover from this.

The other operation is a pectineal resection; removal of part of the pectinious muscle. This stops some of the inward pull on the leg. The operation sometimes produces spectacular results within a few days.

A Hip Dysplasia Scheme is run jointly by the Kennel Club and the British Veterinary Association and dogs may be submitted for X-ray scrutiny between the ages of one and six years. For a fixed price, your veterinary surgeon takes an X-ray of the dog's hips, with the dog lying on its back, with its hind-legs stretched backwards, and its registration number placed on the plate. The X-ray is sent to the British Veterinary Association to be examined by three scrutineers. In Great Britain, the dog is either passed or failed for reasons stated. If the dog is almost normal, a Special Breeder's Certificate may be granted. This is done at the age of two years. In Scandinavia and the U.S.A., the hips are graded 1 − 4, showing the degree of severity. Dogs are normally bred from only if clear, but bitches are sometimes used if Grade 1 or 2.

Osteochondritis desicans

This is a shoulder injury of young dogs usually between five and fifteen months of age, where there is a small, depressed fracture of the bone in the head of the humerus. The cartilage above the fracture slips off and falls into the joint capsule of the shoulder. The injury occurs most frequently in really energetic puppies and is diagnosed by the dog taking small steps with the lame leg and feeling pain on extension of the leg. The condition may settle down or it may require an operation to remove the floating pieces of cartilage.

Sprains of the shoulder muscles, and the muscles on the inside of the thigh are very common. If the painful muscle can be pin-pointed, it helps to massage it gently with soap liniment for five minutes a day, or with white oils for two minutes a day, wiping off the excess liniment afterwards so that the dog does not lick it.

Cruciate ligaments are fairly commonly partially or completely ruptured. The ligaments are in the knee or stifle joint, and they normally stabilise this joint. When they are ruptured, the dog limps on the affected leg and usually stands with the toe on the affected side just touching the ground. The ligaments sometimes heal on their own, but an operation is often necessary to stabilise the joint. Arthritis often follows this condition.

Arthritis. This can occur in almost any joint and develops for a variety of reasons. The main ones are previous injury to the joint, or secondary to another condition, such as hip dysplasia. It usually occurs in older dogs and becomes worse in damp weather. It can be eased when bad by giving various pain relievers and anti-inflammatory drugs such as Phenylbutazone. If it is not too severe, the dog is perfectly happy between attacks.

Parasitic Diseases. Dogs may acquire both internal and external parasites from time to time. Some are transmittable to man and it is therefore important to take any suspected case to your veterinary surgeon as quickly as possible.

Bloat or Distension. This is relatively uncommon in Newfoundlands, but can occur in any of the larger breeds. It can be precipitated by exercising the dog on a full stomach, or by allowing it to eat or drink excessively following strenuous exercise. Sometimes it appears to occur spontaneously, for no apparent reason. The condition is frequently fatal and rapid veterinary attention is essential. The dog appears distressed and may attempt to vomit. The abdomen is hard and painful to the touch and grossly distended.

Heat Stroke. This affects dogs in very hot weather. Those most likely to be troubled are fat dogs with a heavy coat. The temperature rises to 106°F or more, the dog collapses and often has some difficulty in breathing, panting heavily with the tongue looking purplish. A veterinary surgeon must be called immediately and in the meantime the dog must be hosed down with cold water. An ice-pack should be tied to the top of his head. This can be made from a plastic bag containing ice-cubes. Dogs usually recover if treated early enough. It is most important not to exercise Newfoundlands on very hot days. They should be walked first thing in the morning or in the cool of the evening. If the dog begins to pant heavily on a long walk, it should not be coaxed to go any further.

Old dogs can sometimes go into a state of spontaneous "heat stroke", with a very high temperature and congested lungs, in colder weather and for no apparent reason. An ice-pack should be applied and the veterinary surgeon called immediately.

Immunisation. Dogs can be protected against four killer diseases by inoculation. These are Distemper, Canine Virus Hepatitis, Leptospira-Ichterohaemorrhagiae and Leptospira Canicola. Vaccines used may contain attenuated virus or killed virus. You should consult your veterinary surgeon about an immunisation programme for your dog. If he is a young puppy, you should know if any protection was given to him while he was in his breeder's care, as this may have a bearing on the timing and type of vaccine to be used by your own veterinary surgeon.

Skin Trouble. Newfoundlands are not normally affected by skin problems, but the nature of their coats can make treatment difficult. Regular and thorough grooming, particularly at moulting times, minimises the risk of skin trouble developing. The causes can be very varied and it worth seeking veterinary advice as soon as you notice anything is wrong, since long-standing infections can be hard to cure.

Ear Trouble. This can be a problem in Newfoundlands, whose thick fur and drop ears make free ventilation of the ear difficult. The causes are varied, but are most commonly grass seeds or ear mites. Early diagnosis and treatment by your veterinary surgeon are important. Chronic ear trouble, unless it is properly cleared up, may be difficult to cure without surgery. A healthy ear canal should look pale pink and the folds should be small and not swollen at all. There should be no smell. Never poke at your dog's ears with forceps or wooden orange sticks covered in cotton wool, as much damage can be done to the delicate skin inside the canal.

Poisons

There are many different poisons from which a dog can suffer, including a large number which are new products of the chemical industry. It is often extremely difficult to diagnose the type of poisoning the dog is suffering from. The most common are: —

Arsenic. Found in some weedkillers and fungal sprays. The dog vomits violently and has severe diarrhoea and is very ill. If the dog has been seen to eat the poison, it should be made to vomit by giving one dessert spoon of washing soda to two dessert spoons of water immediately, or taken quickly to a veterinary surgeon for treatment. It should be treated subsequently by a veterinary surgeon in any case, as the animal soon becomes dehydrated. The antidote is "Dimercaprol" (2.5mg/kg every 4 hours for 4 days and then reducing over the next 10 days).

Phosphorus. Found in some rat poisons. The symptoms are vomiting, jaundice and great depression. Again, the dog should be made to vomit quickly if it has been seen to eat the poison, by administration of washing soda and water as above. The dog normally dies in four days with fatty degeneration of the liver.

Strychnine. Found in mole poison. The dog goes into rigid spasms, extending its legs and arching its neck backwards. It lives for twenty-four hours in agony. It is dangerous to make the dog vomit if it has begun to go into spasms as it will set it off into a spasm and it may choke. Dogs sometimes survive if anaesthetised for twenty-four to thirty-six hours.

Warfarin in rat poison. This causes haemorrhages within the body. Tiny haemorrhages may be seen in the dog's gums. It becomes very ill, with muscular pain, vomiting and diarrhoea with blood. Again, if the dog has been seen ingesting the poison, it can be made to vomit with washing soda and water. Otherwise it must be treated by a veterinary surgeon.

Alpha Chloralose. A mouse poison. It take thirty minutes or more to take effect. At first the dog is over-active, then it becomes incoordinated. It then sleeps or suffers a drop in temperature. An emetic, i.e. washing soda and water, should be given during the first thirty minutes then the dog must be kept warm and awake. Sedatives should not be given.

Reserpine. First symptoms are diarrhoea, vomiting and shivering, followed by sleepiness and slow breathing. Symptoms show in half to three hours. Sometimes dogs show excitement four hours after taking the poison. An emetic should be given, then the animal kept warm. Sedatives should not be given.

Metaldehyde. Slug poison. The dog becomes over-excited, twitching and jerking, and then goes into fits within half an hour of eating the poison. If early enough, the dog should be made to vomit, but otherwise have sedatives or an anaesthetic administered by a veterinary surgeon.

Sodium Chlorate. Weed killer. The dog has acute vomiting and diarrhoea and bad ulceration of its mouth.

Lead. Found in lawn dressings used to kill leather-jackets. It is also found in linoleum and petrol fumes. It causes fits. The diagnosis is by a blood test and the treatment is by intravenous injection of Calcium Disodium Versenate.

In all these cases, veterinary advice should be sought without delay.

First Aid

Cuts, if on the legs and feet and if bleeding severely, require a tourniquet applied by tying a bandage tightly above the cut and then putting a pressure bandage over the wound. This is done by pressing a large piece of cotton wool on the cut and bandaging tightly over it. The tourniquet should then be released as it should not be applied for more than ten minutes. The wound should be examined by a veterinary surgeon as soon as possible.

Cuts on the pads, if at all deep, are better stitched, because of the weight of the dog, which is so great that it will spread the cut and it takes far longer to heal.

Cuts on ears often bleed profusely. Friars Balsam, if available, can be put on the cut and the ear flap wrapped in cotton-wool and turned back over the head and bandaged firmly to the head with a good, thick bandage. It should be left bandaged for about four days if it is a small cut. A large cut should be stitched.

Other cuts should have the fur trimmed from around them, be bathed in weak disinfectant and then the dog taken to be stitched by a veterinary surgeon.

Any dog which has been injured in a road accident will be shocked and liable to bite, no matter how placid he may normally be. Care should be taken to ensure that no one is bitten before any attempt is made to move the dog. This can be done either by tying the dog's mouth firmly, or putting a coat or a blanket over its head.

Small grazes can be treated by clipping the fur round them and applying antiseptic cream twice daily until healed.

If there are any bones broken, the affected limb should be kept as still as possible. A large blanket can be used as a stretcher to lift the dog into a car and take it to a veterinary surgeon.

If there is any doubt about possible breaks or internal injuries, the dog should be examined by a veterinary surgeon.

Burns and scalds. Injuries caused either by hot water or direct heat should have cold water applied immediately. The fur should be clipped round them if severe, and antihistamine cream applied.

Chemical burns sometimes occur, usually from tepol, the detergent used in washing-up liquids and shampoos. The chemical should be washed off and the fur over the burnt skin removed, and antihistamine cream applied. If the burns are at all severe, veterinary attention should be sought.

Accident with toys. Large breeds of dogs should never, ever, be given tennis sized balls to play with, as they can become lodged in the back of the dog's throat and asphyxiate it. If an accident with a ball does occur, the dog must be rushed immediately to a veterinary surgeon who can quickly administer an anaesthetic and remove the ball. It is extremely difficult to extract it without an anaesthetic as the dog is in a panic and the ball slippery. It can sometimes be done, if one is lucky, by squeezing it out by holding it above the larynx on the outside of the neck and trying to "milk" it forwards, if a veterinary surgeon cannot be found.

Bee and wasp stings. The stung part may swell considerably. If a bee sting, it may be seen and removed, then bathed with a solution of bicarbonate of soda and water. If a wasp sting (no sting is left in), it should be bathed in vinegar or lemon juice. A "Jiff" lemon is very handy for this.

If the origin of the sting is unknown, the part can be rubbed with a cut onion. If the swelling is severe and the dog appears very ill, veterinary advice should be sought.

A two-week old litter of Mapleopal puppies

"A Newfoundlander must not be an awkward, slouching animal, but smart, active and full of life and go — looking at all times ready to perform his duty — to enter a rough sea."

T.E.Masfield 1899

Ch. Harlingen Safe Harbour, owned by Mrs Pat Handley
photo Sally-Anne Thompson

Ch. Sealord of Sparry, owned by Mr and Mrs Aberdeen and shown winning
Best of Breed at Crufts in 1957
photo Fox

Ch. Sea Urchin of Sparry, owned by Mr Cassidy   photo **Cooke**

Ch. Bonnybay Nona of Sparry, owned by Mr and Mrs Lucas and shown winning Best of Breed at Crufts in 1961   photo **Sport and General**

CHAPTER SIX

Colour Inheritance in Newfoundlands

by

DAVID BLYTH

"If you want to be a pioneer, you had better take up something else. At this time, the trick is to play with the cards that have already been dealt."

Johan Pieterse

All the evidence that has been obtained by scientists over the past fifty years indicates that the inheritance in all but the lowest forms of lie is passed on by the bodies known as chromosomes.

These consist of spiral-shaped chains of protein — each link in the chain being known as a gene. They are capable of splitting along their whole length, so producing two exactly similar chromosomes and, as the plant or animal grows, this normally happens, so that each new cell has exactly the same chromosomes as that of its predecessor.

However, with the production of sperms or eggs, this division does not take place in the same way so that each sperm or egg only receives half the number of chromosomes of its predecessor cell.

Thus when the sperm and egg fuse, two half sets of chromosomes are brought together and the new cell formed has the same number as the normal animal or plant.

The usual number of chromosomes for the higher animals and plants is therefore an even number consisting of a number of similar pairs and one from each pair is derived from the mother and one from each pair from the father. On the formation of eggs and sperms the chromosomes pass at random — one of each pair going to each egg or sperm. Thus the egg or sperm will, in respect of each pair of chromosomes in the parental make-up, contain one which is originally derived either from the father or from the mother of the animal producing the sperm or egg.

Since the genes are carried in the chromosomes and when the chromosomes split longitudinally they produce exactly similar genes, normally it follows that every new embryo will have in each pair of its chromosomes one derived from the father and one from the mother. Therefore, it will have one of each parent's genes throughout its entire make-up, but it will only pass on one of these to its progeny.

The actual inheritance of the observable characters of the creature depends on the exact nature of its genes. For example, a particular gene can take several minor modifications and each one affects the appearance of the creature that contains this, so we now have a position in which the creature contains two genes — one derived from the mother and one from

74

the father, which are in the same position on the chromosomes and are very similar, but may not be exactly alike.

When they are not exactly alike, it is usual for one to have a more powerful effect on the appearance of the creature than the other, and when it is almost totally superior in strength to the other, it is known as dominant and the other one as recessive. Where one is considerably stronger, but not totally so, it is known as partially dominant.

All the above is a simplified version of modern genetical knowledge, but it covers the points we need to know to enable us to understand colour inheritance in Newfoundlands.

The Newfoundland Standard says they may be of any colour and it is almost certainly true that, in the past, there were a great many colours represented in the Newfoundland breed, but today the most common colours are black or white-and-black. I have found in the inheritance of the dogs that I have bred, and this has been confirmed to be by observations from other breeders, that black is a simple gene almost totally dominant over Landseer. The consequence of this is that if the dog possesses two black genes it will be black. If it possesses a black gene and a Landseer gene it will be black with usually some small white marks, such as a fleck on the chest. If the dog possesses two Landseer genes it will be a Landseer.

It follows that the pure black dog can only produce sperms carrying the black gene and the pure Landseer can only produce sperms carrying the Landseer gene, whereas the dog that is carrying both genes and appears to be nearly black will produce an equal number of sperms carrying Landseer or black genes. Therefore pure blacks mated together can only produce black puppies; pure Landseers mated can only produce Landseers but Newfoundlands carrying both genes mated together will produce on average one pure black, two apparent black animals with mixed genes and one pure Landseer.

Blacks mated to animals carrying both black and Landseer genes will produce on average half pure blacks and half of black appearance carrying both genes. Landseers mated to apparently black dogs carrying both genes will produce half Landseers and half apparent blacks, which carry both genes. Landseers mated to pure blacks will produce all black dogs apparently, but carrying both genes, on average in both cases.

I feel sure that many breeders will think of exceptions to this which they will quote, but I have never found an exception and Herr Walterspiel of the Schartenberg kennels, who has bred hundreds of dogs, tells me of no exception in his experience. I can only think that the exceptions which may be quoted have come about in some other way which, if fully investigated, could be explained within the system of inheritance expounded above.

Whilst the laws of inheritance of black against Landseer are fairly simply defined in this way, there are several modifications of the main colours which call for comment.

In the pure black which does not carry the Landseer gene, it is still possible to have some white markings, particularly a small vertical line on the chest, and possibly other marks which bear no relation to the Landseer gene, although they look like the markings one normally finds in a black animal which carries the Landseer recessive gene. My knowledge and experience of breeding blacks is far too limited to have any ideas of the inheritance of these minor white marks, except to be confident that they do not have any connection with Landseer markings and no amount of selection for this mark will produce a Landseer.

In the Landseers there are three modifications or points that deserve consideration. The first of these is the inheritance of the pattern of black and white. Consideration of this and a discussion with Professor Robertson of Edinburgh University, who has had a wide experience of inheritance in cattle, in which he tells me that he thinks there is no inheritance of pattern in black and white Friesian cattle, leads me to think that it is almost certain there is no inheritance of pattern in Landseers.

The point Professor Robertson makes is that, if the pattern were inherited, the left and right sides of the animal would show great similarities, whereas with random distribution this would coincide much more with what we observe.

It would, therefore, seem that Landseer marking is the inheritance of the ability of dividing cells, particularly when the embryo is very small, to change to produce black or white colouration, and this takes place at random so producing a random pattern. It is, of course, only a random distribution in the sense that certain parts of the animal are more likely to remain black and certain parts are more likely to remain white than other parts, so that Landseers as a whole tend to have a pattern such as white feet, end of tail, chest and if there is white on the head the most likely point is a white blaze or part blaze down the muzzle.

Similarly, the most likely black areas are round the ears and base of tail but, within these rules which are really something to do with the basic make-up of the animal and not inherited individually, the pattern is random.

The next matter to consider is the question of how light or how dark a Landseer is and this clearly is inherited but not in as simple a way as the straight single gene inheritance of the black against Landseer. Professor Robertson suggests, and my own experience agrees with his view, that it is almost certainly due to a number of genes each adding to the effect of the other. He thinks there are about four. The effect of this would be that when inheriting four of the dark modifying genes an animal would be a dark Landseer, whereas one inheritiing four of the light modifications would be a light one, and those bearing mixed modifying genes would be intermediate.

A little thought will show that, if this is the mechanism of inheritance, dark Landseers would tend to get dark progeny and light ones would tend to get light progeny, but because of the dominance of one form of gene over the other it would not exclude the possibility of light parents having a few dark puppies in their litter and vice versa.

This so well coincides with all the experience I have of seeing Landseer litters that I think this is almost certainly the correct interpretation of the laws covering this aspect of Landseer inheritance.

The third point which modifies the colour of Landseers is the frequent presence of dark grey or black flecks in the white areas. These are never present in the young puppy and only develop at a few weeks of age, and I feel quite sure that they have no connection with the Landseer gene, because Landseer markings are present at birth. I have not sufficient experience to give any ideas as to how this flecking is transmitted.

In Holland, there are a number of bronze Newfoundlands. Those I have seen were dark chestnut with light ends to the individual hairs, as though they had been treated with henna. These dogs may result from a mating of two black parents, and there would seem to be very little doubt that this colour is recessive to black and, therefore, would be transmitted in exactly the same way as the Landseer colour markings. Very rarely, grey Newfoundlands are born, but their numbers are too few to establish a pattern of inheritance.

It is interesting to speculate on the possible part colours of Newfoundlands and also the combinations of colours that could be produced if one wished even today. For example, presumably the Landseer and brown and grey genes are on different places on the chromosomes, and if so, it would be possible to produce grey-and-white and brown-and-white Landseers. In fact, the colour markings would tend to be more like the Pyrenean and it is possible way back that these genes are of the same origin. However, this would be a pointless exercise, because Newfoundland breeders have long accepted the black or white-and-black dogs as the most desirable type.

Mr. Wildman's 'Leo'

Ch. Harlingen Sandpiper, owned by Mrs Hamilton-Gould

Ch. Achates of Fairwater, owned by Mrs C. Handley   **photo Cool**

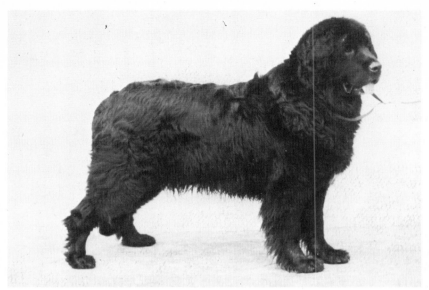

Aus. & Eng. Ch. Bonnybay Jasmine, owned by Mrs J. Gibson

Ch. Bonnybay Mr Barrel, owned by Mr and Mrs Lucas and shown winning Best of Breed at Crufts in 1965 **photo Cooke**

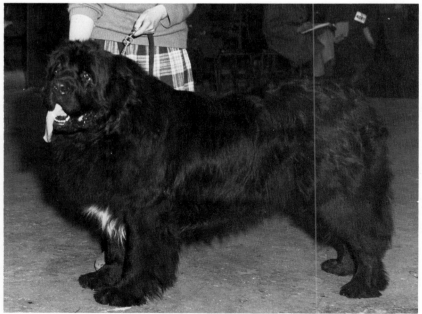

CHAPTER SEVEN

Handling the Stud-dog

by

Miss M. CRUMP

The Newfoundland, along with a few others in the Giant Breeds section, has its own little problems at mating time. He is built for strength and at the same time is loosely assembled. His height is gained mainly from a huge, barrel-shaped body, with great depth, rather than length of leg. This does make things less than easy until the dog learns how to go about his job.

If you intend using your young dog at stud, you should start conditioning him mentally early on. First, he needs to be dominant by nature without being too aggressive. Never make him feel less than "Boss Dog" amongst his own kind, as this is nature's way of keeping the stock strong in pack or herd-living animals. A timid or apologetic male is rarely a success at stud, even in a domestic environment. He must, of course, be under your discipline but this should be firm, not harsh. This breed is so sensitive to praise or blame, that checking him early on for mounting another dog, in the playful way young dogs have, may implant a feeling of guilt when you offer him his first bitch. Instead, he should be called to you, and his attention diverted. Young animals have to learn this way about the facts of life.

Your dog should be used to seeing other dogs and bitches in his garden, but don't let any snap-happy bitch have a go at him, if he should want to find out which sex she is. As he grows older and more masterful, he can put her in her place. Attending a show-training class greatly helps to socialise a dog, if you have only one at home.

Let your young dog be well-grown and starting to mature when you use him at stud. Mating too early can cause a dog to stop growing upwards, and start to mature more rapidly. Fifteen months is usually a good time to try him, but before you do, decide where he is going to do his work. It helps a lot to keep to the same place, as you then build up excitement in the dog when you take him there. The keener the better, as these giant breeds are not noted for a strong sex-drive. A half-hearted dog is going to be very heavy going for everyone concerned.

An empty shed, with good light, or a stable is suitable. Preferably, it should have its own run attached. If you are really pushed, you can use the kitchen, but *do* see that the family is out for the day. Also make sure that the floor is covered with a non-slip material. Quietness is all-important, as the dog must not be distracted. When he has done several services he will be deaf to all outside happenings!

Please don't just put a dog and bitch into a shed, hope for the best and "let nature take its course". It could result in nothing. Worse, the dog could be ruined, by being thrown, if he tries to mount a rough or unwilling bitch. He is unlikely to be presented with an old, experienced female, capable of showing him the way. If he does manage on his own, you may find yourself with a dog who later refuses to mate a held bitch. His first service is a mile-stone in his life and can set the pattern for his future behaviour.

Try to get two friends the dog knows and likes to come as helpers. Let him grow used to them standing either side of him in his mating room. The bitch is usually steadied at the head by the owner, who should be in a position to brace himself against the wall, so that he can support the animal firmly. If the owner is not present, try to make sure there is another helper there to do this.

Your dog should have a strong, plain leather collar (no matter what he usually wears) and you should notify anyone bringing a bitch that she should have one too. Choke chains and slip collars are no good for this job. If the bitch's owners are inexperienced, make sure they have not been dosing her with Amplex or some similar product beforehand.

You will also need a screw-top jar of white Vaseline, some 3″ wide, non-adhesive bandage, a pair of blunt-ended scissors and a piece of strong, fairly thick material, preferably dark-coloured and about 4′ x 2′. Lastly, your "Secret Weapon", one of the major helps in getting a good "tie". This is a platform 3′ long by 2′ wide, made by laying 3′ boards closely together across 2″ x 1″ battens, set in about 8″ from the ends. The boards should be 1″ thick, making the platform 2″ high altogether. It must be firmly constructed, using either screws or strong nails, and covered in hair-cord carpet or something similar. The platform can be used either for a bitch, if she is very small, or for the dog if he is presented with a tall bitch. See that the centre of the board is where the dog will stand, or his weight may tip it up on one end.

It is often difficult to be quite sure when a bitch is really ready to be mated. If she tries to get out to find a dog, she will probably be "Bang on" and should be tried with the dog that same day. An experienced dog knows accurately when a bitch is ready for service, and some refuse to take any interest in any which are not quite there. This is a great help, as your chances of getting a litter from the service are higher when the dog tells you it is the right day.

Now comes the day! Put all your nerves to bed and fill your mind with the feeling that all will go well, otherwise you might transfer your fears to the dog. He should meet his bride with an empty stomach, except perhaps for an egg beaten in a little milk about an hour beforehand. He should also have had a run, to give him a chance to empty his bladder. Remember to put on his leather collar.

If he is to be mated to a visiting bitch, he should meet the owners first, while the bitch remains out of sight. He should show some excitement when he scents the bitch on their clothing. Then shut him away while the bitch is taken to the run outside the mating-room and allowed to ramble around and relieve herself. Put both animals on their leads and introduce them. If they seem friendly, let them both loose in the run, so that they can play and court each other. If the dog tries a mounting, bring the bitch into the room, leaving the dog outside.

With absolutely clean hands, insert a good helping of Vaselene in the vulva (the meaty exit from the vagina). Lift this up on the 1st and 2nd fingers towards the anus, which will make the vulva open slightly, If the bitch is an old hand at the game, she may do this for you. Unless the vulva is in this position when the dog attempts to enter, he will be unable to achieve a clear run into the vagina and may cause the bitch some pain. The owner or one of your helpers should be in a comfortable position, holding the bitch's collar. He must make sure that she does not start to leap about at the moment when the dog's penis swells inside her, producing the "tie". This will be the moment when it is vital to make sure that nothing untoward happens to your much-loved dog. He is at his most vulnerable and totally unable to help himself. A bitch who is in pain or resentful of what is happening can buck like a horse in her attempts to throw the dog off, causing him pain and possible serious injury.

Having made sure everything is ready, with your two handlers standing quietly either side of the bitch, ready to support her if she sags under the weight of the dog, you bring the dog in. Encourage him gently to mount. He may start by trying at her head, or by lifting one of her hind legs to work on. Patience my friend! He may drive you mad by his antics but resist the urge to call him names, except in the most loving tones. Above all, never shout at him. You must build up his ego, not deflate it. When he starts to mount correctly, slip your hand (as flat as possible) between him and the bitch and gently lift the vulva. Find where the dog's penis is striking. If it is at the right level, try to catch the tip of the penis in the slightly open vulva and he should go in without any further trouble. If he does, quickly and unobtrusively remove your hand and stand behind the dog, pressing with your knees against his buttocks for about three minutes. This is to ensure that, even if he cannot enter the bitch fully because the vagina is too tight, the sperm has the best possible chance of reaching its destination. A full tie is not essential for fertilisation, although it is obviously desirable.

After about three minutes, if the dog has tied successfully, he will want to make the first move towards the turn. He will bring one of his front legs over the bitch's shoulder to join the other one. Shortly after, he will turn his body right round, until he and the bitch are standing tail-to-tail, but still joined together. Be ready to steady him while he makes the turn and make sure that the bitch does not try to pull away from him at this time.

It may be that things do not go quite as easily as this and that you find, because of a size difference, that the dog is not finding the vulva. Do not worry. This is where your platform can help. If the dog is striking below the opening, he needs more height. Place the platform centrally behind the bitch, so that he has room to move a little to right or left without falling off. The platform should be just touching her heels. Unless she is a very tall bitch, he should manage now. If the bitch is small and he is striking too high, turn the platform lengthways and stand her with her hind feet at the back edge.

When your helpers need to support the bitch, they should do so by clasping their hands underneath her. Once the tie is made and the dog has turned, they may use the piece of strong material to hold her up. The handler holding the bitch's head must allow room for the dog to rest his head along her neck and shoulder when he drives in. This is the moment when the handler will be glad he has the support of a wall behind him, to help him withstand the forceful push of the dog.

Unfortunately, not all bitches are co-operative at these times. You will have to rely on the dog to tell you if the bitch is ready for mating or not. If he is keen, but she remains resentful, she should be muzzled to avoid the risk of damage to the dog or your helpers. The sweetest-natured bitch can behave irrationally if she objects to being mated. This is when you will need the bandage. Cut a length of about 2 yards. Place the middle of the strip across the bitch's nose, about half-way down, and cross the two ends under and over once. Then take the two long ends each side of the face and tie them firmly behind the head. The bandage must not be so tight as to cause any distress, but it is useless if it is too loose. The moment the bitch ceases to resist the dog, the muzzle may be removed. Using the scissors cause less disturbance to the animals than trying to untie the knot.

There is no set time for a tie to last. Some are over in a few minutes. Others may last up to half-an-hour. When your dog comes away from the bitch, put him out in the run for a few minutes, to see to himself. Then look at him and see if the penis has returned fully into the sheath. If not, very gently pull the sheath back, fill a sponge full of clean, tepid water and trickle the contents over the penis. When the sheath is released, the penis should retreat on its own. Leave the dog to rest quietly and be sure that he has plenty of cool water to drink, as he will be thirsty after his exertions.

The bitch should also be offered a drink and then put straight back into her owner's car, so that she does not have an opportunity to urinate too soon after service.

One last word of warning! Never let yourself be talked into lending your dog to anyone, and do not allow anyone to handle him at stud who has not been trained in your own method of handling.

Editor's Note

If your dog has made a reasonable effort to mate the bitch, without any success, it is better not to persevere without first asking a vet to check that the bitch is fit for mating. If she is a maiden, there may be a physical bar preventing the dog's entry. To continue in these circumstances will only result in an exhausted and frustrated dog, and a hurt and frightened bitch. Furthermore, human nature being what it is, in the absence of veterinary opinion to the contrary, your dog will be blamed for the failure.

You will, of course, have reached an agreement with the owner of the bitch about the stud fee, before the actual mating day. Remember that payment is for a service — not for a litter. Most stud dog owners will allow a free return if no puppies result from the first mating, but there is no legal obligation to do so. If you wish to take a puppy in lieu of a fee, be sure both parties know exactly what the arrangements are, and if possible put everything into writing, to avoid later misunderstandings.

Try to ensure that the first bitch your dog mates is quiet and not a maiden. It is worth offering a free service to an experienced bitch, who has already had one or more litters, to "prove" a young dog. If you wish to advertise your dog at stud, once he is a proven sire, remember to offer him to "approved" bitches only. Without this qualification, you are obliged by law to accept any bitch which comes along. It will do your dog's reputation as a sire no good at all if he is known to have fathered mediocre puppies, even though they come from a bitch of poor quality. He will still be held responsible for them. So it pays to be choosy and make sure that your dog mates only with bitches of a good standard and suitable bloodlines.

Mr Mapplebeck's 'Leo'

Ch. Cherry of Littlegrange and Harmonattan Okay, with their owners Mrs Warren and Mr Morgan, and judge Mrs Roberts   **photo Cooke**

Ch. Sea Gipsy of Perryhow & Ch. Harlingen Coastguard, together with their owners Mrs Shapland and Mrs C. Handley, and the judge Miss Herdsman   **photo Cooke**

Ch. Faithful of Littlegrange, owned by Miss Davies

Ch. Drift of Littlecreek, owned by Mr Cassidy and shown being awarde
her first CC at the age of 14 months by the famous Dutch breeder M
Pieterse
photo Coo

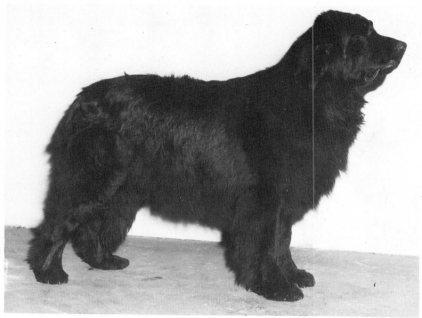

Ch. Littlecreeks Son of Rex, owned by Mr Cassidy   **photo Cooke**

Storytime Figurehead of Esmeduna & Ch. Black Jet of Littlegrange, with their owners Mr Whittaker and Mrs Warren, together with judge Mr Morgan   **photo Cooke**

Ch. Mossie of Littlecreek, owned by Mr Cassidy   photo **R.W.Harper**

Suleskerry Steersman, owned by Mrs Sutcliffe   photo **Ward**

CHAPTER EIGHT

Showing and show-preparation

"Looking at a good Newfoundland should be like looking at a first-class cob."

T.E.Mansfield, 1899

Showing your dog can be fun, as long as your never take it too seriously. You must accept that you cannot win every time, and that you will not always be beaten by better dogs than your own. You will have to learn to tolerate occasional criticism and unkindness. You may comfort yourself with the knowledge that the latter usually come from the least well-informed. Showing can be expensive, and if you are really bitten by the bug, it may mean you have to give up some other luxuries. Never count on winnings to cover your expenses.

You will make lasting friendships. You will be judged, not by your social or financial status, but by your sportsmanship and the way you present your dog. You will learn far more about your dog and its care than you will ever glean from this or any other book. You will discover that, if you are in trouble of any kind, doggy people are second to none when it comes to rallying round and helping.

Having decided you want to show your dog, try to go to one or two shows without him first of all, to see what goes on. The two dog papers carry advertisements, giving the dates of shows. Newfoundlands are not natural show-dogs, and are as likely to roll over and ask the judge to tickle their tummies as pose gracefully. So watch how exhibitors make the best of their dogs and try to decide which style of presentation appears to be most successful. When the judging is over, wander around the benches and ask any questions you like. Most people are only too happy to talk about their dogs and explain how they tidy them up for a show.

Shows are also good places at which to look round for doggy equipment. The trade stands often carry a wider range of things like extra-large collars and leads than a local pet shop can manage.

Send off for some schedules and enter your puppy for one or two shows. You can exhibit him any time after he is six months old, but Newfoundland puppies rarely look up to much at such an early age, and it is probably worth waiting another two or three months, or even longer if he is one of the really slow-maturing kind. Accept that your first few shows will only be training runs anyway. If you enter in that spirit, any wins that do come your way will be a pleasant bonus. Send your entry off in plenty of time. There is little point in entering your pup in any of the senior classes. Classifications vary from show to show, but any championship show scheduling Newfoundlands will offer a class suitable for your young novice.

In order to exhibit your dog at Crufts, you will first have to qualify him with placings at other shows. The conditions for qualification can vary from year to year. Details are available from the Kennel Club.

Your dog must be fit, if he is to have much success in the show-ring. He should, in any case, be fit if he is to lead a normal, active life. Fitness is not achieved by a few days of frantic exercise, taken just before a show. It is the result of a gradual build-up of work. Regular exercise is good for both of you and should be enjoyed equally. If you cannot find time for it, then why bother to own a dog at all?

A puppy does not need strenuous walks. His bones and muscles are not sufficiently developed to withstand the stress. After six months of age, you may start a regular routine of short walks on the lead, combined with free exercise. If you have a large garden and another dog for him to play with, that will probably supply all the galloping he needs in the early stages. Never allow him to become exhausted. Every puppy's needs are different and if yours seems gangling and slow to develop, be prepared to give him extra time to grow.

By the time the dog is about fifteen months old, he should be having at least an hour's free running, plus twenty minutes of road-work. The latter is vital, if he is to build really firm muscles, and if his feet are to be kept in good order. Road-work is the only form of exercise which will harden the pads, keep the nails short and strengthen the dog's pasterns. Any hard surface will do, although it is believed that a rough track makes the dog use his muscles more. These road-walking sessions are when you can teach your dog to walk briskly, on a loose lead. Never allow him to tow you along.

If you have the opportunity to exercise the dog alongside a horse, he will grow exceedingly fit, but remember not to push him too hard. He is not really designed for sustained periods of fast work. He will also need more food, containing a higher ration of protein than normal, if he is to maintain a good appearance.

It is illegal, in Britain, to exercise a dog alongside a car or bicycle on a public road.

Never allow a dog to run around violently just after he has eaten or drunk anything. He may end up with stomach torsion, which is generally fatal, if you do. At best, he is likely to have cramp, which is painful and frightening. Try to make sure that he always has his main meal of the day after he has had his exercise time, and do not feed him immediately after he has taken strenuous exercise. Allow at least an hour for him to settle down.

Your dog should be used to being handled by strangers, and to mixing with other dogs, before he goes to his first show. This is best achieved by taking him to training classes of some kind. You may be lucky enough to have a ring-craft training club in your area. If not, there is almost certainly an obedience class held in the locality. They are often advertised in the local papers, or the Kennel Club can supply details. If you take your dog to obedience classes, explain to the instructors that your dog is intended for the show-ring, so that he may be taught to stand, rather than sit, on command. When the dog is more experienced, it will be useful to train him to sit, but in the early stages it is better not to confuse him.

Practise at home, preferably with the help of a friend. Work out together the pace at which your dog moves most gracefully. Newfoundlands generally look well if they are shown at a brisk walking-pace, or a slow trot. They have a tendency to pace, moving both legs on the same side like a camel, which should be corrected. Sometimes just moving the dog at a faster walk will make him move properly. Otherwise you will have to make him break step, by unbalancing him slightly, either by pushing him off a straight line, or by a gentle, sideways tug on the lead. Do not allow pacing to become a habit, because it is very difficult to break.

Ask your friend to move the dog for you, so that you can view him from the judge's angle. Practise standing him. He should adopt a natural pose, with his weight evenly balanced between all four legs. His attention should be on you, as you stand a little way in front of him. His lead should be slack. Do not stand too close to him, or he will tend to look up to you, with his head pushed back towards his shoulders, giving the impression his neck is very short. If you stand too far in front, the dog may lean forward and spoil his balanced appearance. When you go to shows, you will see a number of people crouching or kneeling down, apparently supporting their dogs from below. This does not indicate that their dogs are cripples. Newfoundlands simply do not see much point in standing still in the same position for very long. It sometimes helps to keep them happy if the handler stays close and perhaps rubs under the dog's chin, or his tummy. You must devise the method which suits you and your dog best. Some easily become bored. Others remain interested in the proceedings. When you practise standing the dog, ask your friend to pretend to judge him a little. His teeth should be examined, so that he is used to having his mouth felt. He should be used to having a hand pressed down on his hind-quarters. Many judges do this, to satisfy themselves that the hips are not weak.

These practice sessions should never last very long. Ten minutes is probably the maximum necessary, if you are doing them regularly. They should be fun, even though the dog has to learn to do as he is told.

Try, if possible, to give the dog some experience of walking on different surfaces. Newfoundlands easily panic, if they feel their feet may slip from under them. Never force your puppy onto a slippery surface. This will simply increase his fear.

The night before your first show, your dog should have been thoroughly groomed, and everything for the next day prepared. Your car should be fit for the road and you should have worked out your route in advance. Both you and the dog should have an early night, though this is a blessed state rarely achieved by even the most experienced of exhibitors, who generally find themselves hunting for some vital piece of equipment at midnight.

Travel as light as possible. Show car-parks are sometimes a long walk from the benching tents. Be prepared for a change in the weather.

Unfortunately, not everyone who attends dog shows is as honest as they might be. Every show, particularly the larger events, has its quota of pick-pockets and sneak-thieves. So reduce the valuables you have to carry to the minimum and never leave property unattended on the bench.

Whether he has been fed or not before you leave for the show, the dog will appreciate a little something during the day. Most dogs are too excited to eat much, but something light will probably be welcome. A raw egg, beaten into some milk, with a spoon-full of honey or glucose added, is ideal. Never give him a bone to chew on the bench. It will almost certainly lead to trouble with his neighbours.

Having arrived safely at the show-ground, the first thing you should do is allow your dog to stretch his legs and relieve himself. If the show is in a city centre you should have stopped at some suitable open space beforehand, for the purpose. Then find your tent and settle your dog and belongings. This is not the best time to start a long chat with fellow exhibitors, who will probably be busy putting a final polish on their dogs. Save the socialising until later in the day. Give the dog a drink. He will find everything very strange and exciting, but try to settle him quietly and on no account allow him to interfere with other dogs. It is not very kind to leave him unattended on his bench for long spells, particularly when he is new to showing and does not understand what is going on.

When you go into the ring, try to be as calm as possible, and if you are in any doubt about what you should do, ask your neighbour or one of the ring-stewards. Do not talk to the judge, except to answer his questions. If you can, avoid standing first in the line of dogs waiting to be seen by the judge. This will give you a chance to see how he is examining the animals, and also how he wants them moved in the ring.

When your turn comes, he will want to go over the dog, either before or after he has seen him move up and down. He will want to know how old your dog is, and will look at his teeth. He may ask you to show the latter to him. In which case, it is not necessary to display all the teeth. The judge only wants to see the front ones. He will not be amused if you inadvertently place your thumb across them, so just draw the lips back gently, and make sure you have kept your head out of the way as well. When you pose the dog before the judge, make sure the hair and skin round his neck are lying smoothly. All your careful preparation will be spoilt if they are bunched up into a tight collar or slip-lead.

After the dog has been seen, stand quietly at the side of the ring and allow him to relax a little, but do not permit him to be a nuisance to other dogs. Keep an eye on the judge and be ready to stand your dog smartly, if he seems to want to take a second look at him. Just as the last dog is being seen, pose your dog, making sure that there is plenty of room all round you, so that you are not interfering with anyone else. If the ground slopes, and it seems to at most shows, point your dog up the slope.

Try to start your dog's show career at some of the out-door summer events. Indoor shows, particularly the smaller ones, can be very crowded and frightening places for a Newfoundland puppy. Wherever you show, your manners and those of your dog are important. If the latter barks endlessly, or constantly attempts to fool around with other exhibits, neither of you will remain popular for long. In the ring, obtrusive chatter with fellow exhibitors will irritate and distract both them and the judge. When the judging is over, congratulate those who have won. If you have been fortunate, accept your win gracefully. As you grow more experienced, you will discover that the most consistently successful exhibitors are also the quietest and most self-effacing.

Grooming

by Mrs FRANCES WARREN

Care of your dog's coat starts from the day he enters your home. Most breeders start grooming their puppies early, so he should already be used to being handled and brushed.

Wherever possible it is best to have a grooming table, so that the dog is brought up to your height. An ideal size is about 2' high, with a wooden top approximately 28" x 36". A slippery surface is not suitable as, should your puppy slip and feel insecure he will be frightened, and it will be very difficult to persuade him to go on the table again. It is bad for young dogs of the giant breeds to jump on and off even small heights, so try to design your grooming table with some kind of ramp. Covering both the table and the ramp with an old piece of carpet will give your puppy a good foothold.

While it is important that the puppy should like being groomed, never make a game out of it. What can be funny when he is a baby can be very different when he weighs over 100lb. So be firm but gentle and teach him that, once he is up on the table, he must not fool about.

The main tools you will need are a fine wire brush with a wooden handle, a strong metal comb, a soft bristle brush, trimming scissors and a stripping knife. Be sure that the comb in particular is a good quality one. Cheap ones are often poorly finished and the teeth can damage both the dog's coat and his skin.

A Newfoundland's coat is not difficult to maintain and if groomed regularly both you and your dog will enjoy the exercise. Regular care makes frequent bathing unnecessary. Washing removes the oil from the coat, making the hair soft and fluffy, and robbing the dog of his natural protection from cold and wet. If you are preparing for a show, bath the dog at least five days beforehand, to allow the oil to return and the coat lie flat. A fluffy coat is incorrect and could well cost you a place in the ring.

A correct coat consists of long, coarse (but not rough) guard hairs, known as the top coat. The undercoat is very dense and soft, almost woolly. This is the layer which protects him in very cold water and

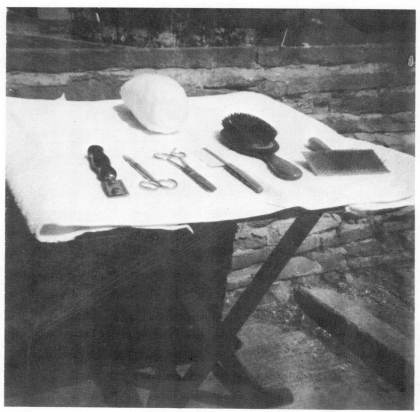

Grooming tools

extremes of temperature. You will notice the first time you bath your dog how difficult it is to wet him right through to the skin.

Good grooming has great advantages. Not only does it keep the dog clean and looking nice, it also helps to prevent skin trouble. Dirty, matted hair will not allow the air to reach the skin and in time can cause wet eczema and sore patches which, if neglected, can be very difficult to clear. Spending just 10 minutes a day will keep his coat in fine condition. If you fail to groom, especially when he starts a spring or autumn moult, he will soon become matted. It is no pleasure to either of you to spend hours removing knots and matted hair. Don't just take a brush or comb and brush your dog quickly from head to tail. You are only grooming the surface and a Newfoundland's coat needs more than that, because of the thick, woolly layer.

To start with, stand your dog on the table and, using the wire brush, brush him all over in the opposite direction to which the hair lies. Then, beginning at the tail end, with one hand pressed against the dog, hold as much hair back as you can handle, showing the dog's skin. Then carefully, layer by layer, brush the hair back into its proper position, making sure you take only as much as the brush can penetrate. When you reach the front legs, work upwards to the chest, making sure you pay special attention to the insides of the legs. Do not forget to brush behind the ears. They are easily over-looked and can become badly matted in a short time. If your dog will lie down it is much easier to do the belly and sides. Remember all the time to be sure you have done each part thoroughly. To finish, use the soft bristle brush and take long, smooth strokes in the direction in which the hair falls. Whether you intend to show or not, he will look and feel ready to take his place with the best.

The metal comb should only be used to help tease out tangles in the feathering and to remove dead hair when the dog is moulting. If you do have to deal with tangles, hold the hair firmly between finger and thumb, as close to the skin as possible. Then work through the knot gently, starting at the end and moving inwards. Always pull against your finger and thumb, to avoid hurting the dog.

Trimming

Newfoundlands need very little trimming, but they do need to have their feet, legs and ears tidied up.

All the dead hair should be removed from the feet. To do this, push the hair between the toes upwards with your fingers and then cut it off neatly. Remove any excessive hair round the pads. If your dog has plenty of roadwalking, his toenails will naturally be worn down by the hard surfaces. If they seem too long, they can be clipped with a nail-clipper. Be very careful not to cut the quick, which is impossible to see if the claws are black. If you are in any doubt, ask your vet to show you how to do it. A safe alternative is a fairly broad-bladed, double cut, metal worker's file. This should be used little and often, always working from the upper surface of the claw downwards, to avoid any tendency of the nail to split.

On the front legs, trim the feather away from the base of the foot and shape the hair up to the heel button. On the back legs remove the hair from the pads upwards for about an inch. Shape the rest of the feathering up to the hock, being very careful not to remove too much. Just tidy the rest of the leg, leaving no long, straggly hairs.

The ears should be covered in neat, short hair, without any hanging below the lower line of the ear. To remove excess, take the thinning scissors and take off all the hair below the line of the ear. Then cut off the rough hair until it is short and tidy all over the flap. Be careful not to remove too much at the top, as that will upset the balance of the head. Take great care while doing this, as it is very easy to pinch and cut the skin with thinning scissors. Finish with a stripping knife to obtain the smooth look which is correct. Sometimes it is necessary to remove excess hair from under the ear, so that it lies close and flat to the head. Always remember to do a little at a time. It is better to take off to little than too much. You can always do more tomorrow. Even if you do not show your dog, keep his ears tidy. They are far less likely to become dirty or infected if the air can circulate round them. If necessary, clean the inside of the ear flap with cotton wool dipped in warm water and then squeezed fairly dry. Use a clean pad for each ear. Never use anything pointed inside the ear and do not even try to push your finger tip into the canal. Do not put any kind of powder into your dog's ears, unless specifically prescribed by your vet.

Practise is the only way to obtain a correct trim, so if you are going to show your dog, start trimming some months beforehand to allow for mistakes.

Early loss of teeth is not a problem in the breed, as it so often is in toy dogs. Raw marrow bones are excellent for removing tartar or plaque which may accumulate, or a monthly rub with a mixture of salt and bicarbonate of soda can be used to keep the teeth white.

The Larger Newfoundland

Ch. Harlingen Wanitopa Moonlight, owned by Mrs Roberts

Ch. Storytime Black Pearl of Esmeduna,
with her owner Mr Whittaker

photo Cooke

Ch. Seashell of Littlecreek, owned by Mr and Mrs Symes   **photo Windsor**

Ch. Lord Hercules of Fairwater, owned by Mrs C Handley and with her grandson Roland   **photo Anne Cumbers**

h. Sigroc King Neptune and Ch. Merikarhun Fay of Sigroc, with
heir owner Miss Davies **photo Kentish Express**

Ch. 'Pied in Crime of Esmeduna, owned by Mrs Poor

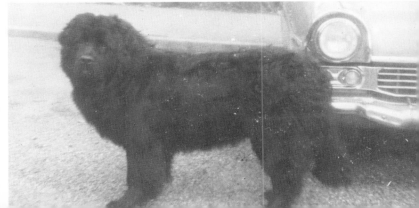

Ch. Bear I Do Love You of Esmeduna, with his owner Mrs Whittaker
photo Cooke

Ch. Attimore Aquarius, owned by Mrs Denham   **photo Diane Pearce**

A Rescue in the Thames

CHAPTER NINE

Working Newfoundlands

Although the Newfoundland is now kept almost solely as a family pet, he has a very long and honourable history of service to mankind. His forebears, living first with the Beothuk Indians and later with early European settlers, were very valuable to their owners. Primarily, they were used for hunting, and very possibly for food themselves, when game was scarce. Later, as larger dogs began to develop from combined native and imported stock, they were used more for draught purposes. The Indians used them chiefly as pack-carriers, or worked them in the travois. The latter was an arrangement of two long birch poles, lashed together at one end. The joined ends were harnessed across the dog's shoulders and the other ends left to trail on the ground behind him. Baggage, or even a papoose, was supported between the poles. It was possible for a dog to pull a considerably greater weight than he could carry on his back.

As time passed, increasing use was made of teams of dogs, pulling sledges. They were to play a major part in the development of Newfoundland, where horse-power was both limited and costly. The country's chief natural resources were timber, fish and seals, and as their exploitation progressed, the use of the dog teams increased. Fish would be carried inland or moved about on the docks, where it was salted and packed. Seal-skins had to be transported. In the summer months, dogs were sent inland to collect loads of timber. It was a hard life for the Newfoundland, and many did not live very long. Frequently, their sole diet was rotten fish and what they could scavenge. It seems incredible that these dogs, which were often vital to their owner's survival, were so poorly treated. It was, however, a

91

'J. S. Rolph's design for the first postage stamp to feature any kind of dog

régime which ensured the survival of the fittest, and was probably to some extent responsible for the fixing of a definite breed-type.

As the fishing industry grew, sailors and dockers became more and more aware of the value of a dog which could swim well and retrieve quickly. Soon, Newfoundlands were being carried on board as ship's dogs, and they were used to carrying lines ashore, as well as acting as rescuers and retrievers when men or equipment went over-board. Much of the fishing was carried on from rowing-boats called Dories, working from larger, sister ships. In all the activity and bustle, as the fishermen hunted along the Grand Banks for cod, there must have been much for a resourceful Newfoundland to do.

With dogs employed in many other settlements around the island, as well as St John's, it is not difficult to see that they made a very considerable contribution to the country's economy. It has been said that just one Newfoundland dog could earn sufficient through the winter to support his owner. There cannot be many other breeds of dog of which this may be said.

As the settlement of the island continued, and the need for basic public services grew, the Newfoundland acquired another important role — as postman. Teams of dogs were used to deliver the mail to out-lying stations in areas that were impassable to horses. In winter, they were able to use frozen rivers as roadways, but at other times of the year they would have to struggle through marshy regions capable of swallowing-up a horse and rider. They have continued into the present century as part of the country's postal system. In recognition of this fine record, the breed has been featured on a number of postage-stamps.

The first stamp issued was the $\frac{1}{2}$ Cent Rose of 1887. Believed to be the first to feature any breed of dog, the stamp was designed by J.S. Rolph of Toronto, and printed by the American Bank Note Company of Montreal. It is thought the model was a dog called Watch, belonging to Henry Duder, the Hon. Harold Macpherson's grand-father. Its appearance certainly owes more than a little to Edwin Landseer.

Newfoundlands did not re-appear on stamps until 1931, when Ch. Westerland Sieger, owned by Harold Macpherson, was featured on a 14Cent issue. The same design was used again in 1937, on the Coronation Long, printed to commemorate the coronation of King George VI. This is believed to be the only time a dog has shared pride of place with a reigning monarch. The stamp was slightly modified and re-issued in 1941.

The French dependencies of St. Pierre and Miquelon brought out their own stamps in 1932, and again in 1941, showing an all-black dog. They also produced a most attractive stamp in 1938, showing a team of four dogs with a sledge. Their most recent stamp featuring a Newfoundland was the 50-Franc issue of 1957.

14 Cent stamp showing Westerland Sieger

While the Newfoundland was valued chiefly as a draught animal on one side of the Atlantic, he was making his mark as a gun-dog in Britain and other parts of Europe. The Encyclopaedia of Rural Sports in 1875 recommended him as an outstanding gun-dog for almost all purposes, but most particularly wild-fowling. Twenty years earlier, Edward Jesse had written, "For finding wounded game of every description, there is not his equal in the canine race and he is a sine qua non in the general pursuit of wild-fowl." In 1854, Youatt also described the breed as fearless in the manner in which they would penetrate the thickest cover. He also stated that generally only the smaller, black dogs were used, the larger variety being more admired solely for their beauty and the different colours with which they are marked. Other 19th Century writers referred to a preference for smaller, dark-coloured dogs, which were less likely to disturb game. It was not long before these dogs were to be accepted as separate breeds, and the Flatcoat, Curly-coated and Labrador Retrievers came into being.

Nevertheless, the Newfoundland is probably still capable of working with the gun and it is a pity that no modern owners seem interested in trying their dogs in this way. They have excellent noses and beautifully soft mouths and their relatively slow pace and unexcitable temperament should suit them well to the rough-shooter.

Until the end of the commercial sailing ship, Newfoundlands were carried round the world as ship's dogs. In Britain, they were popular in many small ports, particularly those where boats were launched from the sea-shore. These boats depended on teams of horses, specially kept for the purpose, to pull them out onto the water, or haul them ashore. Dogs were needed to carry the tow-lines to land, and where no ship's dog was kept, they would swim out to collect the line from a deck-hand. It may seem stranger today to think that boats should be launched or beached in such a manner. In fact, until comparatively recently, there has been a long-established coastal trade round Britain, particularly in the South-West and Welsh regions, using shallow-draught boats, specially designed for the purpose. These little sailing ships traded in and out of tiny sea-ports, often little more than a natural shelter and a beach. Road connections, such as we know today, were almost non-existent and many essential supplies could be more economically delivered by sea. Grain, coal and building materials were all carried in this way, as well as fish and other goods. So it is easy to see that a substantial number of Newfoundlands must have been making their own small contribution to the country's economy.

In areas where seine-netting was carried on from the beaches, dogs were also used to pull the nets in. There are still people alive today who can remember seeing dogs working at the fishing-nets at Slapton Sands and other Devon fishing villages.

The life-saving capabilities of the Newfoundland are well-known. Most present-day owners can testify to the fact that their dogs still possess the instinct to rescue people from water. This can even be irritating at times, when a family simply want to enjoy a swim and find themselves being persistently pushed or pulled back to dry land, even by a dog which has never been taken swimming before. While there have been many isolated instances of dogs rescuing humans, and even other dogs, from drowning, it is not so well known that they have from time to time been officially appointed as life-savers. Teams of dogs, known as "Chiens Plongeurs", were kept on the banks of the Seine in Paris, at the turn of the century, and were regularly called upon to pull people, usually would-be suicides, from the river. At the present time, dogs have been trained to work on some of the major tourist beaches in Brittany, where they have been taught to rescue in pairs. They are also being used experimentally by life-guards on one of the larger beaches in Australia.

From the start of organised breeding and showing in this country, owners have run water-trials for their dogs, to try and ensure that the life-saving instinct was preserved, even though the need for it had dwindled. Some of these contests were arranged in conjunction with shows. Rawdon B. Lee wrote cuttingly in 1899 that, "Such proved neither popular nor interesting, and in one note-worthy case, a much-lauded dog refused to enter the water at all. The last competition of the kind was at Aston, near Birmingham, in 1882, where the best water-dog was undoubtedly the late Mr Bagnall's Landseer Prince Charlie, which won a first prize, a Bedlington terrier being his most formidable opponent."

Water trials are now held annually by the Newfoundland Club. Although they are principally designed to provide an enjoyable day out for the dogs and their owners, it is possible to test a dog's capabilities in the water to a high standard. All dogs competing are initially required to pass a simple test to show their willingness to enter the water and swim to their owner in a boat, a short distance from the shore. Having done this satisfactorily, they may compete in a series of more advanced tests, designed to prove their ability to rescue a drowning person, tow a boat, and retrieve objects from both on and under the water. Nearly all the dogs pass the preliminary test, and many complete the remainder, despite the fact that the majority do not have the opportunity to practise water work at home. Although water-going abilities seem to be more strongly developed in some blood-lines than others, most breeders can congratulate themselves that their dogs still retain the basic instinct to swim and rescue.

Newfoundlands have distinguished themselves in two world wars. In the 1914-1918 war, Col Richardson pioneered the use of war-dogs for various purposes. His "trainees" consisted of a remarkable miscellany of pedigree and mongrel animals, among them a number of Newfoundlands. They were trained for a variety of duties, including running messages between the trenches and guarding property. Col Richardson's book on war-dogs shows a sentry on guard duty, together with a black Newfoundland. The breed was also used for carrying equipment and ammunition. Many medical teams used dogs, not only to carry supplies but also to locate wounded men. Less tangibly perhaps, the dogs must have brought a little

Ch. Storytime Whaler, Mr and Mrs Henry's dog
photo Sally-Anne Thompson

affection and comfort to men who found themselves pitchforked into hell.

In the Second World War, the British use of dogs was largely confined to the more popular working breeds, such as Alsatians. The American and Canadian forces, however, did make use of the Newfoundland, mainly as a pack and draught animal. Mixed teams of Pyreneans, Huskies and New-foundlands were used for cable-laying in snowy terrain where more conventional methods could not be used. They carried the drums of cable on their backs, while their handlers paid it out behind them. A soldier, writing later of his experiences with the dogs, recorded that they thrived in the bitter cold. Each dog was provided with his own kennel to sleep in. Each morning, when their handlers went to fetch them, they found that the majority of dogs were lying outside, virtually buried in the over-night snowfall and apparently perfectly warm and happy.

Dogs have not been used for draught purposes in Britain since it was forbidden by law in 1850. While the legislation was necessary to prevent much abuse, it is perhaps a little sad for the Newfoundland, who enjoys pulling a cart or sledge. It is still permissible to let your dog pull a small load on your own property.

Attimore Moby, owned by Mr and Mrs Peter Oriani, this dog won the Water Trials in 1969 and 1971   **photo Welwyn Times & Hatfield Herald**

Although play-acting would never be regarded as real work by a New-foundland, a mention might be made here of one or two who have earned distinction as actors. Carlo was included in a production at the Theatre Royal, Drury Lane, in 1804. The script required him to plunge into a tank of water and rescue a damsel in distress. The young lady was clad in an elaborate Elizabethan costume and there is no record of the wardrobe mistress's comments about this nightly performance, which must have caused her a great deal of work. An anonymous writer commemorated the part played by Carlo in verse:

> No actor great in histrionic name
> Than Carlo boasts a prouder, nobler fame:
> E'en Garrick, Nature's favourite child, must yield
> Nature HERSELF with Carlo takes the field.

It is not known how long the production lasted, or whether it perhaps enjoyed a revival, but fifty-two years later C.Machey wrote a few lines about the event:

> Ho! Carlo! Newfoundland! go, follow his cry,
> As it graspingly answers the seamoaner's sigh;
> The boat shall be lowered, the men shall belay —
> Life-saver! Wave-stemmer! Deep-diver! Away!

Two other Newfoundlands achieved star status more recently, in 1976, when Mr and Mrs Harding's Hamish and Robbie (Sea-lord Amish of Aston and Ch.Gentle Bear of Aston) appeared in Ibsen's "When We Dead Awaken" at the Crucible Theatre in Sheffield. According to both critics and cast, they played their parts perfectly.

In the last few years, Newfoundlands have found themselves in a very different role, as drug-detectors. They are now employed by the Canadian police at two air-ports, and have been trained to stand quietly by any baggage containing narcotics. As soon as the owners of the bags claim them, they are arrested.

Although the Newfoundland is no longer needed by man as a working dog, he is still capable of being usefully employed. His instincts and willingness are there. In particular, with ever-increasing numbers of people trekking to our beaches each summer, his inherent desire to save life could be more widely used.

Training and working with your Newfoundland

by

Mrs J. GIBSON

"Any Dogges may be most notable curres, according to their first ordering and trayning: for Instruction is the liquor where-with they are seasoned, and if they be well-handled at the first, they will ever smell of that discresion, and if they be ill handled they will ever stink of that folly."

Gervase Markham, writing of training water-dogs in 1621

There are many excellent books on the controversial subject of dog-training and this is not intended to deal with it in depth. However, there are a number of pitfalls for the novice handler to avoid, and also some special aspects to the training of a Newfoundland, which is capable of very varied work.

The main obstacle to having a well-trained dog is normally oneself. Tuition for the owner, and the ability to absorb and then pass on information to the dog is difficult. The best way of learning these things is to go to training-classes. Join a local club. There are hundreds throughout the country and the Kennel Club can provide you with details of any in your area.

Go for the initial visit without the dog. This will enable you to make contact with the trainers and secretary, who will want to tell you the times of their beginners' class and also the type of equipment you will need. You will probably need a good leather lead about 6′ long and a chain-linked training collar — sometimes incorrectly called a choke chain. This collar is not in any way cruel. Correctly fitted on the dog, it loosens automatically the moment any tension on the lead is released. With a dog like the Newfoundland, which has a ruff of very thick fur round its neck, it is far more effective than a conventional collar. However, its use should be reserved solely for training sessions, and possibly showing, as it can be dangerous if the dog is running loose. He may be caught-up in undergrowth or possibly catch a tooth in part of the loose chain and damage himself. Chain collars are particularly hazardous if two dogs are playing together.

Apart from learning to do various exercises, training-classes are excellent for your dog's manners. He will learn to meet and behave sensibly with other dogs of all shapes and sizes. Before all training sessions, the dog should have been carefully exercised, to prevent fouling of the training area.

In his book "Training Dogs", Col. Most places great emphasis on the mistake of anthropomorphism in dog training. It is easy to fall into this

Correctly positioned slip collar. Put on in this way, the collar loosens as soon as tension on the lead is relaxed

error — investing dogs with human attributes. Remember, the dog does not understand the meaning of an order. Therefore, simply to command it to do something is a waste of time. It must be realised that any threat of punishment is useless. So is a correction after the event. The remark so often heard, "Look at the remorse on his face", is the owner fooling himself. The dog's expression is caused by fear, induced by the owner's tone of voice. This same owner will still expect the dog to come to him when called, even as he threatens.

To be a good handler, one has to understand the nature of the dog.

Each has a different personality and traits can run in families. It is sometimes difficult to judge how much compulsion each particular animal requires. A cross tone of voice can be more hurtful than a flick with a stick to a dog with a hard temperament. The owner must learn how to achieve rapid changes in the tone of voice, so that the dog can be corrected the moment he errs, but also be praised lavishly the instant he corrects his behaviour.

Puppy Training

A litter of puppies can learn much while they are still in the nest. Their first lessons will be from their mother, who will teach them to respond to the call for dinner. This is the start of learning to come when called. She may also teach them to relieve themselves on newspaper later on. When the puppies are bigger, games of retrieve and hide-and-seek become useful initiation exercises for adult work. Any natural attribute, such as the pup which shakes paws with you, is worth encouraging. At quieter moments, teach the puppies to stand still and allow you to brush them gently. They should also be encouraged to lie down for grooming. Never have a puppy on a slippery surface during these early sessions together.

Simple obedience can start at about five months, but preferably not for more than five minutes each day. Above all, the puppy must enjoy himself. If he becomes bored or frightened by your lessons, you are in deep trouble. It has been calculated by scientists working on animal behaviour that a top-class working Alsation dog has the reasoning-power of a $2\frac{1}{2}$ year old human. This may seem hard to believe, when we can see incredible work by police and service dogs at displays round the country. But what we see is mainly the result of sympathetic and repetitive training, rather than any super reasoning on the dog's part. So never expect too much of your puppy. In particular ,Newfoundlands are not canine master-minds, even if they do have a tremendous desire to please, so patience and kindness are all-important.

Miss Brooks' Sailor retrieving a dummy at the Water Trials   **photo 'Dogs Life'**

Esmeduna's Happy Result of Orovales, owned by Miss Yeoward, 'rescuing a stranger'. This bitch has won the Water Trials once and came second in her only two attempts **photo Heswall & Neston News & Advertiser**

To show their willingness to enter the water **photo 'The Star'**

Robert Wilkins receiving extra assistance from Plaisance Tillicum, while Harraton's Sea Lily of Pendragon tows him ashore   **photo 'The Star'**

A suitable carting harness

The first formal lesson your puppy should have is to learn to walk quietly on a lead. If he has never had a collar on before, start just by putting it on and allowing him to become used to the strange feel of something round his neck. He will try to shake it off, or scratch at it, for a while, but pretty soon he will forget he has it on at all. Next attach the lead and let it trail on the ground. You will be using the small, cheap collar and lead which you bought for him at this stage. When he is used to the lead dangling from his collar, you can pick up the end and encourage the puppy to walk beside you. Do not pull him along, and if necessary follow him for a while, rather than try to make him go with you. He will soon grow accustomed to the idea of you walking beside him and then you can coax him to come in the direction you want to take. Do not allow him to pull you along, with the lead in his teeth. Do not let the lesson go on for too long. A few minutes each day will imprint it on his mind far more effectively than an hour or more once a week.

Mr Robinson's Littlegrange's Sea King pulling a 19th Century dog cart made in France

As the puppy's lessons progress, you can start teaching him to walk correctly to heel, on your left side. His nose should be about level with your knee and he should walk along smartly, with his head up. Teach him from the outset that sniffing at lamp-posts and interesting smells on pavements is strictly for off-duty occasions, when he is not on the lead. If he attempts to pull forward or sideways, bring him back into position with a sharp (but not rough) jerk on his collar. The moment he responds, release the pressure on the lead. If you try to keep him in position by maintaining a steady pull on the lead, he will try to fight against it. He must learn that walking beside you is the comfortable thing to do. Always reinforce your actions with the command Heel! Before very long, the word alone should be sufficient to make him walk correctly.

To teach the dog to sit, maintain a steady upward pull on the lead, while

Ch. Wanitopa Matilda, owned by Mrs E. Nix   **photo East Anglian Times**

The Hambledown Fire Brigade   **photo Lionel Young**

at the same time pressing firmly down on the base of the tail. The moment the dog obeys, release the pressure on the lead. While you do this, you will of course command the dog to Sit! Praise him and tell him how clever he is.

With these two basic exercises leant, the dog is half-way to being civilised. If you want him to be a pleasure to own, you should continue his training, at least to the stage where he will stay put on command and come to your call. If you want to try any kind of life-saving or water work with him later on, you should also teach him to retrieve and to "hold" an article in his mouth. Newfoundlands are perfectly capable of reaching competition standard in obedience work, though special attention is needed to make them work smartly.

Many training clubs hold their classes in small village halls, or other places of the kind, which have wooden floors. Even though not well-polished, Newfoundlands can find them frighteningly slippery. If you think this could be a problem with your puppy, try to put in a little practice at home first.

When the puppy wants to swim, let him. They often do so very early, but never tire him and never try to force him to enter the water. Instead, make sure he has a friend more competent than he, either human or canine, to encourage him. He will have a natural instinct to retrieve objects in the water and this should be fostered. A piece of thick rope tied to a small lump of wood makes a good toy to practise with. Not all Newfoundlands will retrieve from under water, but most will try, once they realise what is required of them. When the puppy is confident in the water, weight a favourite plaything so that it will sink to the bottom, and let him see you

The Hambledown Pedlar's Cart

he Hambledown Bakeries

Mr Corderoy's Ch. Clywood's Worthy Boy with his circus van

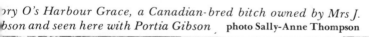

ory O's Harbour Grace, a Canadian-bred bitch owned by Mrs J. bson and seen here with Portia Gibson **photo Sally-Anne Thompson**

drop it in the water. Start off in a shallow place and keep the toy on a length of string, so that you can rescue it if necessary. All swimming exercises are extensions of basic dry-land obedience.

Water-Training and Life-Saving

One of the disadvantages of water training is that it is tremendously popular with all the family. While the puppy and your children may have a hilarious time splashing about in the water, it is unlikely that the dog will learn much. So try to start his lessons in private. A dog whistle can be useful. Do not start the training until the dog is obedient to recall on dry land, as he may become over-enthusiastic and swim out too far for his own safety, if you cannot bring him back on command.

Start with straightforward retrieving. When the dog is doing this well, send him into the water for a "baby". Any old doll which will float will do, though try to avoid using one made of the type of light-weight plastic which breaks easily. If it is dressed, or wrapped in an old towel, it will be easier for him to grab hold of.

Life-saving requires some finesse, because the dog must learn not to damage the person he is rescuing. Lessons should not start before the dog is well-grown and you will need the assistance of a light-weight person who can swim competently. In a real life-and-death situation, the dog might be called upon to rescue either a conscious or an unconscious person. If they are conscious, he should circle round them, to enable them to grasp hold of him. The majority of dogs seem happiest if the "drowner" places an arm across their shoulders, but a few will tow someone holding on to the tail.

Mrs Gwynn with Empress of Littlegrange

108

r Mackintosh with Jonathan and his cart

Mr Shearwood with Gerahmeen Glade of Littlecreek

iss Brooks with Kingfishereach Admiral

On no account should the dog's collar be held, as this might stop him from breathing freely.

If the drowner is unconscious, the dog should grasp him by the upper arm, and either attempt to bring him ashore or simply support him until help comes.

Towing a boat is not difficult, once the dog has been trained to distance control on land. Make sure the dog has something substantial with which to pull the boat. A thin rope will slip through his teeth and possibly hurt his mouth. The rope should have a piece of wood attached to it, to keep it afloat and so that the dog has something firm to grasp in his mouth.

A word of warning, before dogs are encouraged to jump off a dock or a bank into unknown water. Do check for submerged stakes or rocks. Encourage the dog to go in carefully, walking down the bank, rather than plunging. Also, please remember that tragedies have occurred with dogs becoming trapped in steep-sided swimming-pools.

Mr Knight's Hambledown Chief Stoker tows a boat at the Water Trials in 1976. He was runner-up in both 1975 and 1976   photo **Birmingham Mail**

Carting

Many dogs enjoy pulling a cart or a sledge, and their owners can have a lot of fun, while at the same time a sense of purpose may be achieved by using the cart to carry lawn clippings or carry out other similar jobs around the garden. Children love being given rides on a dog-cart, but always make sure someone responsible is leading the dog, unless he is absolutely steady and trained to vocal commands.

The cart should be soundly constructed. A four-wheeled cart, with a front axel which swivels on a central pin, is best, as it is easily manoeuvred. Two wheels are elegant, but the balance is difficult to achieve, because the shafts have to be long and this makes the cart difficult to turn in a small space. The design of the cart can be as simple as you wish, but a number of owners derive considerable enjoyment from making replicas of horse-drawn vehicles and displaying them at Newfoundland Club "Fun" days or local charity events.

The harness need not be elaborate, but it is essential that it fits correctly. Remember that your dog's measurements can vary according to whether he is carrying a winter or summer coat, so see that the harness allows for considerable adjustment. The breast-girth must be wide and thickly padded. Sheepskin or thick felt are suitable. The neck-strap should be capable of being moved forward or backward for comfortable chest width. A bitch weighing 100 lbs will need a front-piece between the two ends of the neck-strap of about 11″ − 12″, a larger dog will need more. Any competent saddler can make a harness for you. Preferably it should be made from good-quality leather, which you keep in supple condition by frequent applications of saddle-soap. Remember a Newfoundland's coat is

Miss Chadwick with Uskrail Kentish Ann, winner of the 1976 Water Trials and placed on many other occasions **photo Birmingham Mail**

111

Slip-chain

Double-slip

Bench chain

very soft, and hard leather can soon rub a sore place. An alternative to leather is the strong nylon webbing which is used to make halters for horses.

A dog should not be allowed to start carting exercises until it is twelve months old, when you may begin with a log weighing about 14lbs, attached to the harness with a ring-bolt. Make sure that the dog is not so close to the dog that it bumps against his heels. Proper carting may be started when the dog is about two years old. Begin the dog's training on level ground and only introduce him to working on a slope when he is fully confident. If the dog is going to have to control a loaded cart on a downward slope, fit some kind of breaching-strap, to prevent the cart from pushing the harness up round his shoulders. You should, in any case, be prepared to act as a brake.

Voice control is not difficult, if you and the dog have already attended training classes and achieved a reasonable standard in basic obedience. The commands are simple; halt, forward, stay, sit, back, left and right. Start training with the dog on collar and lead at first, even if he is normally steady off the lead.

Working Trials
Newfoundlands have achieved very little in Working Trials in this country, although they have done a certain amount in America and Australia. The breed is not physically designed to compete with more athletic types of dog which can manage the Regulation jumps of 9′ long and 3′ high, plus a 6′ scale. However, they are perfectly capable of undertaking tracking work and will enjoy doing so.

In all training, remember patience, firmness and kindness are essential. Preface all commands with the dog's name. This ensures that you have his attention when you wish to give him an instruction. The first dog is the one which really teaches his owner, but the knowledge gained is with you for ever.

One, Two, Three

Ch. Highfoo Harraton's Ocean Queen, owned by Mr Winston

photo Diane Pearce

Ch. Your Sweet Bippy of Esmeduna, owned by Mrs Warren

Harraton's Sea King, owned by Mr Frost

...h. Cascar Merikoira, with his owner
...rs Sharpe's daughter

photo Kentish Times

Ch.Laphroaig Attimore Aries, owned by Mrs K. Gibson

Ch.I'm Dimpy Too of Esmeduna with her owner Mr Whittaker, winni
Best of Breed at Crufts in 1972   **photo Diane Pear**

Ch. Uskrail Faroes, owned by Mr Jeferies

Ch. Esmeduna's Annalisa of Sigroc, owned by Miss Davies **photo Diane Pearce**

The Newfoundland by Philip Reinagle

CHAPTER TEN

The Artist and the Newfoundland

"The Distinguished Member of the Humane Society"

by Sir Edwin Landseer

Because of his relatively recent development, there are no ancient paintings or sculptures of the Newfoundland. There are stone and bronze statues of retriever-like dogs, dating from pre-Roman times. There are also mastiffs dating from the same period. A most impressive example is the "Dog of Alcibiades" dating from approximately 400 BC and owned by the Earl of Feversham. This carved stone mastiff is shown as a smooth-coated dog, but his head and ears are covered with fairly long, curly hair, which gives him a remarkably Newfoundland appearance. However, while these statues may represent early ancestors of the breed, only the most optimistic could claim them as undisputed Newfoundlands. The same must apply to very early paintings. Some writers have tried to claim the dog in "Procris Dead" by Piero di Cosimo (1462-1521) was a retriever. Although he is dark-coloured, his appearance suggests more of the hound.

In 1607 Topsell illustrated a dog of Portuguese Water Dog type in his "History of Foure-footed Beastes". Sir Peter Lely painted Sir Philip Sidney accompanied by a collie-like dog which, according to the de Lisle family records, was a Newfoundland. The first recognisable example of the breed was probably Thomas Bewick's woodcut of Mr Liddell's dog at Eslington,

114

in Northumberland. This was made in about 1789 and the accompanying text shows that Bewick knew the breed well, as he referred particularly to the dog's webbed feet and his ability to retrieve under water.

Philip Reinagle's engraving of about 1800 shows a better-looking dog by modern standards, giving an impression of strength and agility. Although the dog is white-and-black, some versions of the engraving show a team of four all-black dogs in the background, pulling a load of logs down to the sea-shore.

W. Taplin's "The Sportsman's Cabinet" of 1803 included pictures by Rysbrack and Pugin, as well as the Bewick and Reinagle engravings. Barker-Daniel's "Rural Sports" included prints by Stubbs and Gilpin. In 1830 John Ferneley (Snr) painted his family at their Melton Mowbray

*The marble dog 'Bashaw' sculpted by
Matthew Wyatt*

photo Victoria & Albert Museum

home. They are accompanied by a large, woolly dog, not unlike Ben Marshall's dog, painted in 1811. Ben Marshall had painted another New-foundland before, a black puppy called Satan. Satan's long legs and lack of coat give him the look of a Great Dane.

Sir Francis Grant's painting of "The Earl of Litchfield's Shooting Party", dated about 1840 included a group of gun-dogs, one of which was black with lighter shadings and a wavy coat. Stonehenge, in "British Rural Sports" published in 1867, used an engraving taken from a painting by G.

An interesting pair of Parian figures made by D.C.French in 1872, entitled 'Imposing on Good Nature' and 'Retribution'

Earl. The Victorian painter R.Ansdell painted a group of a Scottish sportsman and three dogs, in a Highland setting. One of the dogs is a black Newfoundland with tan points and a white chest. Another dog is almost entirely white and his size in relation to the man suggests that he too is a Newfoundland. The third dog appears to be an Irish Setter. A significant detail is the mixed bag of game spread on the ground. It emphasises the Newfoundland's popularity as an all-round gun-dog in the last century.

The famous French painter Renoir included a white-and-black Newfoundland in his portrait of "Mme Charpentier and Her Children" in 1879.

The best-known painter of the breed must be Sir Edwin Landseer (1802-1873), whose name became indelibly associated with the white-and-black variety. His painting of "A Distinguished Member of the Humane Society" is undoubtedly his best of a Newfoundland. The "Distinguished Member" was in fact a stray, named Bob, who reputedly saved many people from drowning in the Thames, before his adoption by the Humane Society. Although the painting commemorates his courage, the model used was another dog called Paul Pry.

Sir Edwin painted other Newfoundlands, including his own, and "Twa Dogs", which was completed in 1822. However, after the phenominal success of the Distinguished Member, which was widely reproduced and became a great favourite with Victorians, he never managed to recapture the character of the breed. Alcoholism and depression affected his work and in spite of owning a number of Newfoundlands himself, he made the classic Victorian mistake of over-sentimentalising and humanising his animals. Some of the facial expressions in his later paintings were hideous. He was frequently copied by engravers and imitated by less competent artists, generally with poor results.

At the same time as the Newfoundland became a popular subject with painters, he was also frequently modelled and sculpted. There was also a brief vogue in the last century for bronze or cast-iron dogs, often life-size. These appealed more to American taste and foundries in the United States were busy for some years satisfying public demand.

In England, the fashion was more for stone dogs. There is a pair of these guarding the portico of Thirlestaine House in Cheltenham. Unfortunately, there is no record of who carved these statues, but there is another, identical one marking the grave of Nelson at Pythouse in Wiltshire, which suggests that some West-country sculptor had found a successful formula with the owners of big houses.

A design for a Victorian chocolate box lid, painted by Richard Cadbury
reproduced by kind permission of Cadbury Brothers Ltd.

Cut-outs from a Victorian children's book

The dog at Pythouse was obviously a much-loved pet. His memorial stands on a large stone plinth, on one side of which are carved the first four lines of Byron's epitaph for Boatswain. On the other side are the words, "In Memory of Nelson — the perfect Retriever and the most affectionate of friends. He died Oct 21st 1871, on 69th Anniversary of the death of his Illustrious namesake, England's greatest admiral." Not only was Nelson remembered in stone, but his portrait was painted as well. This shows him with his master, together with a hunter and a "St Johns" black dog. Nelson appears to have been quite a tall dog and mainly white. His coat was curly and not very long.

Another dog to be remembered by his owner was Bashaw, who belonged to Lord Dudley. In 1831, Matthew Coates Wyatt was commissioned to make a marble statue of the dog. It was His Lordship's wish that the animal should, "Live to posterity in the breathing marble." Wyatt was extraordinarily successful in achieving this, even though his fee of 5,000 guineas seems large, even by modern standards. Lord Dudley died in 1833, leaving Matthew Wyatt unpaid, and his executors a long and bitter battle over the outstanding debt. Eventually, Wyatt also died and his son sold the marble dog for 160 guineas. It subsequently changed hands two or three times and eventually was acquired by the Victoria and Albert Museum.

SYMPATHETIC ENQUIRIES. C.A.HOLMES.

Serie 62-7894

Newfoundlands

Serie 62-7652

A favourite with the young and old,
Who always is as good as gold.

125

Some Newfoundland cigarette cards

A report in the Court Journal of 1834 describes the statue vividly, "The variegated coat of the animal, even to the minutist marks, is closely copied in the white, black and grey marble . . . . it is only with the greatest difficulty that any joining in the material can be traced. The eyes are composed of gems (the Persian topaz and Sardonyx), the pupils of black lava; and, but that the form is motionless, it might, at a very slightest distance, be taken for life."

The pedestal is elaborately decorated with semi-precious stones and the dog stands on a cushion made of yellow marble. The weight of the dog was such that Wyatt had doubts about the ability of the legs to support it, and cleverly introduced a bronze snake into the composition. The serpent's coils prop up the underside of the animal, whose paw pins it to a cushion. The snake's eyes are reputedly of rubies. The statue is a remarkably life-like creation, as it should be, since Lord Dudley's coachman took the poor dog to more than fifty modelling sessions at Wyatt's studio.

The Staffordshire potteries were also quick to capitalise on the popularity of the Newfoundland, and they soon produced china figures, though never in the numbers which pugs, poodles and spaniels achieved. They were generally decorated in brown and white, possibly because this was easier to produce than black and white in the underglaze paints available then. Although brown and white was an accepted colour for Newfoundlands at that time, it did make the pottery dogs easily confused with St. Bernards, which were then becoming popular. On the whole, the potters did not produce attractive likenesses. They were more successful

127

The Wendy Bronze by Sir Cecil Thomas, OBE, which stands in the Royal Botanical Gardens, Dunedin, NZ

with plain, white Parian-ware models, and with decorated plates and mugs, but they rarely captured the gentle dignity of the breed.

Victorian photographers were also happy to take advantage of the New-foundland's success. Many post-cards were produced, generally showing the dogs in sentimental poses with small children. Dogs with a lot of white on them were favoured, and anyone who has attempted to photograph all-black dogs will appreciate the reason for this. Later, Newfoundlands appeared in collections of cigarette cards.

Other items included coloured cut-outs for children's scrap-books and of course many illustrations for children's books. Sadly, the latter were usually spoilt by the artists' determination to give their subjects humanised expressions. Sometimes, the results were unattractive to the point of ugliness. Nevertheless, they all serve to remind us of the immense popularity of the breed and its very well-earned reputation as good companions for children.

Coming to more modern times, various artists have tried to paint the Newfoundland, without a great deal of success. One exception was Arthur Wardle, whose painting was reproduced in Rawdon B. Lee's "Modern Dogs" of 1899. He was followed by F.T.Dawes, who painted the great Ch.Gipsy Duke in about 1914. Sadly, the original of this lovely painting has disappeared, but a detailed enlargement of the head only was used to illustrate the breed in Hutchinson's Dog Encyclopaedia, published in instalments in the late 1920s. More recently, two Americans, Edwin Megargee and Howard Proctor, have produced excellent Newfoundland portraits.

A special mention should be made of Harry Pettit, who owned Naze Blaze, the first white-and-black Newfoundland to be whelped in Britain

One of a pair of stone Newfoundlands guarding the entrance to Thirlestaine House, Cheltenham College

after the end of the war in 1945. Mr Pettit designed the letter-head for the Newfoundland Club. It is a most attractive composition, suggesting both the kindliness of the breed and its willingness to carry out the dangerous work of saving life.

Present-day supporters of the breed have reason to be grateful to the generations of photographers who have recorded the top dogs, almost from the very beginning of organised dog-shows. The early photographers had many difficulties to cope with, not least the fact that their photographic plates required the subjects to remain motionless for some time. Some outstanding prints were produced by Thomas Fall's studio, happily still photographing dogs today. The present generation of photographers are producing excellent work. A number of them have been able to persuade owners to allow their dogs to pose less rigidly than before, with very happy results.

Ben Marshall and his Newfoundland Dog

Ch. Attimore Minches, with her owner Mrs Randall   **photo Norwich Mercury**

Ch. Clywood's Worthy Boy and Ch. Sigroc Miss Me, with their owners Mr Corderoy and Miss Davies, together with judge Mrs Kempster   **photo Cooke**

Suleskerry Sailmaker of Fairwater, owned by Mrs C. Handley

photo Anne Cumbers

h. Gentle Bear of Aston and Sealord Amish of Aston, with their owner
rs Harding   **photo Sheffield Newspapers**

Tarnhill Lonely Sea and Ch. Tarnhill Sound of Arisaig, with their owner
Mrs E. Powell   **photo Gordon**

Ch. Ragtime Off She Trots, owned by Mrs Eidson **photo Telegraph & Star**

Mr and Mrs Pratt's Hambledown Boatman, with the Newfoundland Club's Challenge Cup **photo Lionel Young**

The Newfoundland Dog — original breed

CHAPTER ELEVEN

Newfoundlands and Writers

If Newfoundlands were not always well-served by artists, they have fared a little better in the hands of writers and poets, even though a number of Victorians managed to endow their work with nauseous sentimentality.

Byron is the most famous man to have both owned and written about a Newfoundland. His dog Boatswain, a black dog with a fair amount of white on his chest and paws, was born in Newfoundland in May 1803. Byron's devotion to him went far beyond normal limits. When the dog died, the poet buried him in the family vault at Newstead Abbey, much to the dismay of his relations. In 1809, Byron made a will, directing that his body should be laid to rest beside that of Boatswain's. The dog died relatively young from a form of madness, probably rabies. Leslie A. Marchand wrote in his autobiography of Byron, "So little aware was Lord Byron of the nature of the malady, that he, more than once, with his bare hand, wiped away the slaver from the dog's lips during the paroxysms." Byron wrote one of the loveliest of all epitaphs for his friend, and had it carved on one side of an elaborate memorial.

> *Near this spot*
> *Are deposited the remains of one*
> *Who possessed beauty without vanity*
> *Strength without insolence*
> *Courage without ferocity*
> *And all the virtues of man without his vices*

This praise which would be
Unmeaning flattery
If inscribed over human ashes
Is but a just tribute to the memory of
Boatswain, a dog
Who was born at Newfoundland, May 1803
And died at Newstead Abbey
November 18, 1808

Byron also wrote the following lines, which express vividly the grief he felt at the loss of his dog.

"Inscription on the Monument of a Newfoundland Dog"—Newstead Abbey, 1808

When some proud son of man returns to earth
Unknown to glory, but upheld by birth,
The sculptor's art exhausts the art of woe,
And storied urns record who rest below;
When all is done, upon the tomb is seen,
Not what he was, but what he should have been;
But the poor Dog, in life the firmest friend,
The first to welcome, foremost to defend;
Whose honest heart is still his master's own,
Who labours, fights, lives, breathes, for him alone
Unhonour'd falls, unnoticed all his worth,
Denied in Heaven the soul he held on earth;
While man, vain insect! hopes to be forgiven,
And claims himself a sole exclusive Heaven!
Oh man! thou feeble tenant of an hour,
Debas'd by slavery, or corrupt by power,
Who knows thee well, must quit thee with disgust,
Degraded mass of animated dust!
Thy love is lust, thy friendship all a cheat,
Thy smiles hypocrisy, thy words deceit!
By nature vile, ennobled but by name,
Each kindred brute might bid thee blush for shame.
Ye! who, perchance, behold this single Urn
Pass on — it honours none you wish to mourn:
To mark a Friend's remains these stones arise,
I never knew but one, and here he lies.

The Scottish poet Robert Burns was well-acquainted with the Newfoundland and described one in his poem "Twa Dogs".

His hair, his size, his mouth, his lugs,
Showed he was nane o'Scotland's dogs;
But whalpit some place far abroad,
Where sailors gang to fish for cod.
His locked lettered braw brass collar
Showed him the gentleman and scholar;
But though he was o'high degree
The fient a pride, nae pride had he.

Lord Byron was not the only person to write a memorial to his Newfoundland. Lord Grenville was also inspired by his love for a dog called Tippo, who came to live with him after swimming ashore from a ship-wreck. The poem was originally written in Latin and was carved on a stone tablet in the grounds of the family home at Dropmore.

Here, stranger, pause, nor view with scornful eyes
The stone which marks where faithful Tippo lies.
Freely kind Nature gave each liberal grace,
Which most enobles and exalts our race,
Excelling strength and beauty joined in me,
Ingenuous worth and firm fidelity.
Nor shame I to have born a tyrant's name,
So far unlike to his my spotless fame.
Cast by a fatal storm on Tenby's coast,
Reckless of life, I wailed my master lost.
Whom long contending with the o'erwhelming wave
In vain with fruitless love I strove to save.
I, only I, alas, surviving bore,
His dying trust, his tablets, to the shore.
Kind welcome from the Belgian race I found,
Who, once in times remote, to British ground
Strangers like me came from a foreign strand.
I loved at large along the extended sand
To roam, and oft beneath the swelling wave,
Tho' known so fatal once, my limbs to lave;
Or join the children in their summer play,
First in their sports, companion of their way.
Thus from many a hand a meal I sought,
Winter and age had certain misery brought;
But Fortune smiled, a safe and blest abode
A new-found master's generous love bestowed,
And midst these shades, where smiling flow'rets bloom,
Gave me a happy life and honoured tomb.

Sir Walter Scott owned Newfoundlands, though his greatest affection was for the Deerhound. Charles Dickens owned two called Don and

133

Bumble. Don, on one occasion, rescued the puppy Bumble from drowning. Dickens later wrote, "The scientific way in which he towed him along was charming."

J.M.Barrie, the creator of "Peter Pan" and the dog-nursemaid Nana, was a Newfoundland owner, although originally Nana was modelled on his St. Bernard Porthos. Curiously, it is a long-standing tradition of this children's play that the dog should be played by a male actor, although nothing could be more feminine than Nana, with her insistence on such unpopular activities as bathing. Nana must be one of the best-known animal characters in children's literature, and she will probably remain a firm favourite with the young, long after such ephemeral creatures as Tom and Jerry have vanished. The Wendy Bronze, modelled by Sir Cecil Thomas, OBE and standing in the Royal Botanical Gardens in Dunedin, New Zealand, has a delightful Nana lying at the base of the statue. The model for this work was Mrs Roberts' Harlingen Taaran Taru. Her whole attitude expresses horror and concern at the sight of the Darling children flying above her. A recent visitor to Dunedin reports that the bronze dog has been polished by the action of hundreds of little hands stroking her. No Newfoundland would ask for more.

Edmund Blunden, one of the best English narrative poets, wrote "Incident in Hyde Park, 1803", describing how a duel was fought over the rival merits of two Newfoundland dogs.

> "And here through the park come gentlemen riding,
> And behind the glossy horses Newfoundland dogs follow.
> Says one dog to the other, 'This park, Sir, is mine Sir.'
> The reply is not wanting: hoarse clashing and mouthing
> Arouses the masters
> Then Colonel Montgomery, of the Life Guards, dismounts,
> 'Whose dog is this? The reply is not wanting,
> From Captain Macnamara, Royal Navy: 'My dog.''
> 'Then call your dog off, or by God he'll go sprawling.'
> 'If my dog goes sprawling, you must knock me down after'."

A very dramatic description of the duel followed. It ended tragically with the death of one man and the appearance of the other in court on a charge of murder. Meanwhile, oblivious of their masters' adventures, the two dogs "Stretched at home in the firelight." The poem closely followed a true incident. Happily, the jury refused to convict the survivor of the duel and he was acquitted.

Newfoundlands regularly appeared in children's books, from the late-Georgian period onwards. They usually featured in "improving" tales or poems. The writing was generally poor and the style sugary. R.M.Ballantine cast one of the breed in a more suitable role, when he made him the hero of "The Dog Crusoe", a splendid tale of the Wild West, written in

1860. A less attractive example appeared in "The Infant's Magazine" of 1877:

ROSIE AND SNOW

A very great pet is beautiful Snow,
With his dear little mistress, Rose;
He stays close beside her to guard and to play,
And follows wherever she goes.

He's a faithful and valued and loving old friend,
Gentle, honest, unselfish and kind;
One MORE true and faithful to dear little Rose,
I know that you NEVER can find.

Hundreds of little poems and stories similar to this were written and must have led to a strange idea of the Newfoundland as a paragon among dogs, with almost super-human qualities of wisdom and nobility.

Towards the end of the Eighteenth Century, two different developments occurred which were to have a considerable effect on the dog world. One was the improvement in the efficiency and availability of sporting guns. The other was that methods of book production changed. The result was that shooting became more generally popular and that books on the subject were written to satisfy a new need. Every aspect of the sport was written about, including the breeding and training of sporting dogs. The Newfoundland figured in many of these books. He was frequently recommmended as the best all-round retriever. Later, he was popular as an outcross with many other gundog breeds. Col. Hawker was among these early sporting writers. He was followed by many others, some of whom widened their interest to cover every aspect of dog-keeping, as well as the history and development of different breeds. W. Taplin's "Sportsman's Cabinet" contained a lengthy and well-illustrated reference to the Newfoundland, as did "Rural Sports", by William Barker Daniel, By the middle of the last century, more generalised dog books were appearing. George Jesse appears to have been particularly fond of the breed and included many stories about Newfoundlands in his "Anecdotes". Although he states that the majority are true, some of them are so far-fetched that one is tempted to speculate upon the origin of the expression "Shaggy-dog story".

Jesse was followed a few years later by Dr. Gordon Stables, "Stonehenge", Vero Shaw, A. Croxton-Smith and James Watson. While none of these people was in the same class as Byron or Scott, they do form an important part of the breed's literature, and cannot be ignored.

Not until the present century, has any non-fictional book devoted to the Newfoundland been written. Shortly before the Second World War, a small book was published in Holland by the famous breeder J. Pieterse. Since then, works by Mrs M. Booth-Chern, Joe Stetson and Mrs Maynard K. Drury have been published in the United States, while from Canada has come a small book by Donn M. Purdy. While all these are most welcome, it would be good to think that somewhere there is a writer capable of putting the Newfoundland back where he really belongs — as the central hero in a first-rate story.

Getting a surprise, by George Cruikshank

Ch. Littlegrange Anna. with her owner Miss Crackle

Ch. Bachalaos Bright Water of Stormsail,
with her owner Mrs Oriani

photo Cooke

Ch. Captain Starlight of Littlegrange And Ch. Ta Ta Maria of Littlegrange,
with their owners Mr and Mrs Warren   **photo Diane Pearce**

Sukiln Puffin and Ch. Greenayre Dogwatch, with their owners Miss
Osmond and Miss Totty, and judge Joe Braddon, at Birmingham National
Show in 1974   **photo Diane Pearce**

Ch. Attimore Royal Sovereign, owned by Mr and Mrs Dorman
photo Diane Pearce

Ch. Barlight Buccaneer of Littlecreek, owned by Mr Cassidy and shown winning his first CC at 8½ months
photo Cooke

Ch.Sukiln Polly Wagtail, owned by Miss Osmond **photo Diane Pearce**

*Mr and Mrs Adey's bronze Newfoundlands, Shermead Brown Beauty an
Shermead Bright and Beautiful* **photo Vernon Brook**

CHAPTER TWELVE

Some Newfoundland Stories

"When affection only speaks, Truth is not always there."

Thomas Middleton

A Drinking Dog

Here is a story I remember of a Newfoundland dog — an immense black, a good-humoured Newfoundland dog, He came from Oxford and had lived all his life at a brewery. Instructions were given with him that if he were let out every morning alone, he would immediately find out the river, regularly take a swim, and gravely come home again.

This he did with great punctuality, but after a little while was observed to smell of beer. The lady was so sure that he smelt of beer that she resolved to watch him.

Accordingly, he was seen to come back from his swim around the usual corner, and go up a flight of steps into a beer-shop. Being instantly followed, the shopkeeper is seen to take down a pewter pot, and is heard to say, "Well, old chap, come for your beer as usual, have you?" Upon which he draws a pint and puts it down and the dog drinks it.

Being required to explain how this comes to pass, the man says, "Yes, Ma'am, but I didn't when he first come. He looked in Ma'am — as a brick-layer might — and then he wagged his tail at the pots, and he gives a sniff round and conveyed to me as he was used to beer. So I drawed him a drop, and he drunk it up. Next morning he come again by the clock and I drawed him a pint, and ever since he has took his pint reg'lar."

Charles Dickens

The Sagacity of Mr Poynder's Dog

Mr Poynder, the brother of the Treasurer of Christ's Hospital, brought home from Newfoundland a dog, a native of that country. This dog had established a strong claim on his master's affections, from the circumstances of his having twice saved his life by his sagacity in finding the road home when Mr Poynder had lost his way in snow-storms, many miles from any shelter: and when his master had embarked for England and had left him in the care of friends at Newfoundland, the dog had swum more than three miles to the ship in order to rejoin him. Mr Poynder landed at Blackwall, and took the dog in a coach to his father's house at Clapham. He was there placed in a stable which he did not leave until the second day of his arrival, when he accompanied his master in a coach to Christ's Hospital. He left the coach in Newgate Street and proceeded through the passage to

137

the Treasurer's house; not being able to gain admittance to the garden entrance, Mr Poynder went round to the front door, and thinks he left the dog at the garden entrance, for he did not recollect seeing him afterwards. In the hurry and excitement of seeing his friends, he for a few minutes forgot his dog, but the moment he recollected him he went in search of him. He was nowhere to be seen, and his master hastened to prepare his description and to offer a reward in the public papers. Early, however, next morning a letter arrived from the captain of the ship in which Mr Poynder had sailed from Newfoundland, informing him that the dog was safe on board, having swum to the vessel early on the previous day. By comparing the time on which he had arrived with that when he was missing, it appeared that he must have gone directly through the City from Christ's Hospital, to Wapping, where he took to the water.

Taken from a book of true dog stories

Maude McKenzie and Juniper

It is just three years ago, at the time I write, and in this same pleasant month of June, that I first met Maude McKenzie, down in one of the flowery lanes of bonnie Berkshire. Surely more than sixteen was that little maiden, and fresh and beautiful as the gowans her feet brushed the morning dew from, as she lightly tripped along. But there was a half-frightened look in her eye as it met mine, which for a moment I could not account for. Frightened she surely need not have been, for trotting along at her side was a trusty friend indeed. Tall as a mastiff this noble Newfoundland, black as wing of raven, the blackness just relieved by the red ribbon of a toungue that peeped from his mouth, and by the rows of alabaster teeth, that he flashed in the sunlight, every time he cast a glance of love and pride upwards at the sweet young face of his mistress. But here, reader, was the cause of her dread. I too had a dog of the self-same breed, Bob to wit, but in consideration of his boundingly impetuous habits, usually known by the name of Hurricane Bob.

I defy anyone, however, to say there is a single atom of vice in Hurricane Bob's disposition; only given any large black dog of his own size, and Bob would fight, Irish-like, for the fun of fighting.

So on this occasion —

"Dear me, now," said Hurricane Bob soliloquizing, but fixing his eyes on the other Newfoundland, "I should like to know whether that dog or I am the taller. I wonder if my good master would mind me running across, to measure shoulders with him?"

"I should mind it very much indeed, Robert," I said. I always call the dog Robert when talking seriously to him. It seems more impressive, you know, than Bob.

"You needn't feel the slightest alarm, Miss," I continued, addressing the young lady, who was kneeling on the ground with both arms around her

Go little letter, apace, apace

favourite's great neck. "I have got my dog securely by the collar. But what a lovely animal you have there."

I frankly confess, I threw in the last sentence for the sake of prolonging the picture for the moment — the kneeling maiden and the beautiful dog. Admiration of one's dog never fails to lead to conversation.

The girl's face brightened in a moment, and the clouds of fear were dispelled.

"I am so glad," she said, "You admire him, but everyone loves poor Juniper." "Juniper!" I said, "What a strange name!"

"Protection, you know," she explained, looking a little surprised, as it were, to meet any person not au fait in the language of flowers.

We met many times after that, Maude and I and the dogs, and had many a pleasant and friendly chat together. Even Hurricane Bob and Juniper learned to behave socially one to the other, and would trot peaceably enough side by side, or romp together on the grass. Maude hardly ever went anywhere without Juniper, and on more than one occasion he followed her to church, where it was admitted by everyone who saw him that he behaved quite like a Christian.

In course of time, and that a very short time too, Maude died, cut down in the flower of her youth by the scourge of our land, phthisis. It was affecting enough in all conscience to see poor Juniper quietly following the funeral. There was some mystery about the matter, that his canine mind couldn't fathom; only he knew it was his duty to watch and follow his mistress; and when the coffin was lowered, and the sods arranged, it was with the greatest difficulty the dog could be removed from the churchyard. Juniper died within a fortnight afterwards, of grief, they said. But I never see a young girl with a large dog as her companion, without thinking of poor Maude McKenzie.

Taken from a collection of short stories belonging to Mrs C Handley's father

A World War I Hero

Just after the start of the war, Harry Henson, chief kennelman for Colonel Wilsher, was testing Jemmy, a four year old Newfoundland dog for water working trials. The trials were tests of the dog's use in various kinds of water work. One of them required the recovery of an object from under-water.

Because of age, the Colonel, Harry and the dog were rejected for active war work, although one of their younger dogs was going. So they were given the task of patrolling the coastline near the Colonel's house. One night, they saw a light out to sea, signalling to someone ashore, who, when spotted by the Colonel, dashed into the sea, carrying a brief-case. The Colonel shot the spy and Jemmy swam out and pulled the body ashore, just as he had been trained to do. A week later, the War Office said that the papers in the brief-case might have cost this country the war, if they had fallen into enemy hands.

Taken from a children's newspaper

Sulla

Sulla was the large, white-and-black Newfoundland belonging to the famous romantic novelist Ouida, whose real name was Marie Louise de la Ramee.

When Ouida stayed at expensive hotels, Sulla always accompanied her. In the hotel kitchens, Sulla's diet caused dismay among the cooks and staff. Ouida and her dog became well-known figures at many of Europe's most expensive holiday resorts. In London, the novelist and her mother frequently entertained Guards officers, on one condition — they had to be dog lovers, for Sulla was always present. Ouida's hand was often sought in marriage, and once to everyone's amazement, she announced that Sulla had won her heart and he was her hero.

Although Ouida was eccentric, she was a great animal lover, and no one escaped her sharp tongue where cruelty was concerned. For years she campaigned for a society to prevent animal cruelty.

When Sulla died in Florence, Ouida had her pet buried in her special dog cemetery.

Taken from "Diana" girls' magazine

The Cleverness of Brian

Brian was a Newfoundland dog belonging to a gentleman named Spratt, who had a fine house near the town of St. Helens in Lancashire. At times Brian seemed as wise as a human being, and, indeed, often Mr Spratt would say, "If all folks were as clever as Brian, the world would be a wonderful place."

Mr Spratt had taught Brian all manner of tricks, and he was fond of showing-off the cleverness of the dog to all his friends. He would take a pack of cards, ask someone to pick out a card from the pack and then replace it. Then shuffling all together Mr Spratt would scatter the pack face downwards on the carpet, and Brian would at once pick out the chosen card.

One evening someone dropped a sovereign upon the floor. The coin rolled away under the furniture, and in spite of a long search by all those present, it could not be found. Brian was sitting on his haunches, lolling out his tongue and watching what was happening with great interest. Presently his master said, "Find it, Brian!" Brian immediately wagged his tail, opened his mouth in a wide laugh, and then raising one of his paws, showed the sovereign lying beneath it.

Mr Spratt often used to give Brian a penny and the Newfoundland would hurry off to the baker's to buy a penny bun. One day, by way of a joke, Mr Spratt gave Brian a bad penny. The dog hurried away to the baker and gave him the penny, but the baker looked at the penny, shook his head, and gave Brian back his coin. For a moment Brian seemed puzzled, and then he turned away and trotted homewards. Coming to his house he hastened to his master, dropped the bad penny at his feet, wrinkled up his nose as if he were sneering and then tossing his head in the air, he walked away.

Many of Mr Spratt's friends used to give Brian pennies, but the dog did not always bring home buns. His master wondered what became of the coppers.

As Brian turned over on his bed one evening, Mr Spratt heard a chink. He went to Brian's bed and began to search. All the while the search was going on Brian growled softly and showed his teeth. At last, hidden under the bedding, Mr Spratt found one shilling and ninepence in pennies. With a laugh his master replaced the coins, and then Brian wagged his tail and went to sleep.

I think this shows that Brian was as wise as most human folk. I'm sure he was wiser than I am, for I never could save my pennies, and I am afraid I shall never learn the way.

From Stephen Southwold's "Animal Stories"

The Watchful Newfoundland Dog

In the autumn of 1869 there appeared in the columns of a Belfast newspaper, "The Northern Whig", the following account of a very wonderful dog. The dog in question is a Newfoundland, the property of a captain who sails one of the steamers running between Belfast and Barrow-in-Furness. The vessel generally makes the trip during the night. As soon as her steam is up "Bob", certain occasions being excepted, mounts to the gangway and takes his place beside his master, or whoever else may be on the look-out. There he sits all through the voyage, keeping a sharp look-out ahead. Whenever the lights of any strange vessel come into view, in the path of the steamer, Bob barks out a loud warning, and should the captain or mate not seem to take any notice by at once shouting out directions to the man at the wheel, Bob keeps on barking until the orders are given, or he is informed by a pat on the head that all is right and that there is no danger to be feared.

However, on exceptional occasions Bob, as soon as he sees preparations being made for leaving harbour, goes on shore, and no entreaties will coax him back on board. Should he suspect violent measures are about to be resorted to, he trots off and disappears into the town. At such times as Bob deserts his ship, the night before the voyage is completed is certain to prove wild and stormy, although there are no signs of rough weather at the time of the vessel's departure. By what exercise of instinct — or may it be termed process of reasoning? — is Bob enabled to foretell the weather, as many other animals do, cats and sheep for instance? Is Bob a coward in deserting his ship, or does he wish to impress upon his master that the voyage he is about to take is fraught with danger and disaster?

Taken from a book of true dog stories

A Fishing Newfoundland

At certain times of the year the streams in some parts of North America not far from the coast, are filled with fish to an extent you could hardly believe, unless you had witnessed it — and now comes the Münchausen story.

A real Newfoundland, belonging to a farmer near one of these streams, used at these times to keep the house well supplied with fish. He thus managed it: he was perfectly black, with the exception of a white fore-foot, and for hours together, he would remain almost immovable on a small rock which projected into the stream, keeping his white foot hanging over the edge as a lure to the fish. He remained so stationary that it acted as a very attractive bait: and whenever curiosity or hunger tempted an unwary fish to approach too close, the dog plunged in, seized his victim, and carried him to the foot of a neighbouring tree, and on a successful day he would catch a great number.

Taken from "Dog Breaking" by Gen.W.N.Hutchinson 1848

Mr Jukes, in his "Excursions in and around Newfoundland" referred to the same dog, or one remarkably like it. According to him, the dog belonged to a George Harvey, and from his description was one of the Lesser Newfoundlands or St John's dogs. The dog spent most of his day diving into the water, which was six or eight feet deep, to catch his fish, and Jukes only saw him "toll" with his white paw when the fish were scarce. He sometimes caught up to sixty fish in one day and was never seen to eat any.

Given the opportunity, alas rare in Britain, Newfoundlands will often attempt to catch fish. They are most effective in shallow water, where they use a combination of teeth and front paws.

Lord Tankerville's Fish

Late in the 18th Century, the Earl of Tankerville accused the Earl of Home of allowing his Newfoundland dog to poach up to thirty salmon from his water each day. Lord Home denied the offence and his neighbour took him to court, but lost the case.

"Tang"

In 1919, the SS Ethie ran aground off Bonne Bay. All seemed lost, when the Newfoundland ship's dog, called Tang, was persuaded to swim ashore with a line. The passengers and crew, numbering ninety-one, were all rescued, including a three month old baby girl, who was slung ashore in a mail-bag.

Napoleon's Escape from Elba

Napoleon's first escape from Elba nearly ended in his death. He fell over-board in the dark and the sailors searching for him in a rowing-boat could not find him. A Newfoundland dog belonging to the men, jumped into the sea and pulled him back to safety.

Westerland Champion

In 1941, the Canadian Victoria Rifles, accompanied by their mascot Westerland Champion, were fighting a desperate rear-guard action against the Japanese in Hong-Kong. A Japanese grenade landed in the middle of a group of Canadians and Champion snatched it up in his mouth and carried it away from them. Seconds later, he was blown to pieces, but his action had saved twenty men's lives.

A Newfoundland at Trafalgar

At the Battle of Trafalgar, in 1805, HMS Nymph's Newfoundland mascot played a captain's part throughout the engagement with the French ship Cleopatra. He remained on deck during the whole of the encounter and when the French ship was finally bested, the first to board her was the dog.

"Watch"

On June 12th 1828, the passenger ship Dispatch, sailing from Liverpool to Quebec, went ashore on a reef off Isle aux Morts, a few miles from Port aux Basques. She had one hundred and sixty-three people aboard and night had already fallen. Distress signals were fired, but on that remote and rocky coast, there was little chance they would be seen. However, one fisherman, named George Harvey did see the flares and set out in his small boat, together with his seventeen year old daughter and twelve year old son and his Newfoundland dog "Watch". When they reached the Dispatch it was to find that they could not approach close to the ship because of the violent surf breaking around it. There seemed to be no chance of taking a line ashore, when Harvey quietly commanded Watch to swim to the ship. The dog fought his way through the water and was given a line, attached to a belaying-pin, which he took back to his master. The Harveys returned to shore and managed to rig a breeches-buoy, on which every person aboard the Dispatch was safely brought to land.

George Harvey and his children received the gold medal of the Royal

Humane Society, a reward of one hundred sovereigns and a letter from the King.

Six years later, Watch made a similar rescue, when a cargo ship, the Rankin from Glasgow, ran ashore in almost the same place. This time, he saved twenty-five people.

Although the name George Harvey is not uncommon, it seems likely that Watch and the dog which used his white paw to entice fish could be the same. If this is so, then his courage was considerable, because Jukes described him as being relatively small and light-framed.

A Dutch Incident

A native of Germany was travelling one evening on foot through Holland, accompanied by a large dog. Walking on a high bank, which formed one side of a dyke, his foot slipped, and he was precipitated into the water; and, being unable to swim, soon became senseless. When he recovered his recollection, he found himself in a cottage on the contrary side of the dyke, surrounded by peasants. The account given by one of them was, that returning home from his labour, he observed at a considerable distance a large dog in the water, swimming and dragging, and sometimes pushing something along that he seemed to have great difficulty in supporting, but which at length he succeeded in getting into a small creek on the opposite side. The peasant discovered that it was the body of a man, whose face and hands the dog was industriously licking. The body was conveyed to a neighbouring house, where proper means soon restored the drowned man to life. Two very considerable bruises, with the marks of teeth, appeared, one on his shoulder and the other on his poll, whence it was presumed that the faithful beast had first seized his master by the shoulder, and swam with him in this manner for some time, but that his sagacity had prompted him to quit this hold, and to shift it to the nape of the neck, by which he had been able to support the head out of the water; and in this way he had conveyed him nearly a quarter of a mile before he had brought him to the creek.

Taken from "The Dog" by William Youatt

Rescue near Aberdeen

Dr Beattie relates an instance of a gentleman attempting to cross the river Dee, then frozen over, near Aberdeen. The ice gave way about the middle of the river; but, having a gun in his hand, he supported himself by placing it across the opening. His dog then ran to a neighbouring village, where, with the most significant gestures, he pulled a man by the coat, and prevailed on him to follow him. They arrived at the spot just in time to save the drowning man's life. Taken from "The Dog" by William Youatt

A Merciful Dog

Dr Abel relates a singular instance: "When this dog left his master's house, he was often assailed by a number of little noisy dogs in the street. He usually passed them with apparent unconcern, as if they were beneath his notice; but one little cur was particularly troublesome, and at length carried his impudence so far as to bite the Newfoundland in the leg. This was a degree of wanton insult beyond what he could patiently endure; he instantly turned around, ran after the offender, and seized him by the skin of the back. In this way he carried him in his mouth to the quay, and holding him some time over the water, at length dropped him into it. He did not, however, seem to design that the culprit should be punished capitally. He waited a little while, until the poor animal, who was unused to that element, was not only well ducked, but nearly sinking, and then plunged in, and brought him safe to land."

Taken from "The Dog" by William Youatt

If the above story seems just a little far-fetched, it is worth recording that Mrs Roberts, President of the Newfoundland Club, wrote of a similar incident in Hutchinson's Dog Encyclopaedia. In this case, Mrs Roberts knew of the dogs concerned.

Another story was told of the Newfoundland and the Bulldog who, in the course of a fight, fell down some steps and into deep water. The Newfoundland was able to scramble ashore, but his adversary was not so fortunate. However, the big dog, apparently deciding to forget their previous animosity, pulled the Bulldog out of the water, and the two dogs became firm friends afterwards.

A Rescue in Kent

A vessel was driven on the beach of Lydd, in Kent. The surf was rolling furiously. Eight poor fellows were crying for help, but not a boat could be got off to their assistance. At length a gentleman came on the beach accompanied by his Newfoundland dog; he directed the attention of the animal to the vessel, and put a short stick in his mouth. The intelligent and courageous fellow at once understood his meaning, sprung into the sea, and fought his way through the waves. He could not, however, get close enough to the vessel to deliver that with which he was charged; but the crew understood what was meant, and they made fast a rope to another piece of wood, and threw it towards him. The noble beast dropped his own piece of wood and immediately seized that which had been cast to him, and then with a degree of strength and determination scarcely credible — for he was again and again lost under the waves — he dragged it through the surge and delivered it to his master. A line of communication was thus formed and every man on board was rescued.

Taken from "The Dog" by William Youatt

Prince Albert's Dog

A noble animal of this kind was presented to the Zoological Society by His Royal Highness Prince Albert. He is a great ornament to the gardens; but he has been somewhat unmanageable, and done some mischief before he was sent thither.

Taken from "The Dog" by William Youatt

Harlingen Viking

Harlingen Viking was exported to Boston, Mass. and then re-sold to a gentleman living in Rhode Island, and became the family pet. By some unknown means a fire broke out in the home, and the dog, knowing instinctively that there was something wrong, warned the family. Viking was awarded a medal for his bravery and the incident was widely reported in the American press.

Told by Mrs Roberts

A Dog from Newcastle

During a severe storm, in the winter of 1789, a ship, belonging to Newcastle, was lost near Yarmouth; and a Newfoundland Dog alone escaped to shore, bringing in his mouth the captain's pocket-book. He landed amidst a number of people, several of whom in vain endeavoured to take it from him. The sagacious animal, as if sensible of the importance of the charge, which in all probability was delivered to him by his perishing master, at length leapt fawningly against the breast of a man, who had attracted his notice among the crowd, and delivered the book to him. The dog immediately returned to the place where he had landed, and watched with great attention for everything that came from the wrecked vessel, seizing them, and endeavouring to bring them to land.

Taken from "A General History of Quadrupeds" by Thomas Bewick

A Tyneside Dog

A gentleman walking by the side of the river Tyne, and observing, on the opposite side, a child fall into the water, gave notice to his dog, which immediately jumped in, swam over, and catching hold of the child with its mouth, brought it safe to land.

Taken from "A General History of Quadrupeds" by Thomas Bewick

147

The Price of an Island

In 1639, a year before either Southold or Southampton was founded, Lion Gardiner explored his little wooded island and purchased it from the Wyandanch Indians. He named it the Isle of Wight (now Gardiner's Island) The price paid included one large, black, woolly dog, one flintlock gun, powder and ball, some Jamaica rum and several Dutch blankets.

Taken from Bailey's "Long Island, Nassau and Suffolk."

A Dog at Tunbridge Wells

A cousin of one of my brother officers was taking a walk at Tunbridge Wells, when a strange Newfoundland snatched her parasol from her hand, and carried it off. The lady followed the dog, who kept ahead, constantly looking back to see if she followed. The dog at length stopped at a confectioner's, and went in, followed by the lady, who as the dog would not resign it, applied to the shopman for assistance. He then told her it was an old trick of the dogs' to get a bun, and if she would give him one, he would return the property. She cheerfully did so, and the dog as willingly made the exchange.

Told by Col Hutchinson some time before 1850

A Newfoundland nearly goes in the Pot

The Lewis and Clark expedition of 1802 was accompanied by a Newfoundland named Scannon, of which the explorers were very fond. The dog acted as the party's retriever, helped kill deer and chased grizzly bears and buffalo from the camp. Even though he ate as much as a man, and sometimes the men were very short of food, Scannon was never grudged a meal. So when he was stolen by the Indians, whose intention appeared to be to pop him into a pot and cook him as soon as possible, his owners were far from pleased. They quickly organised a rescue party and the Indians, when they saw that Scannon's friends meant business, released him without argument.

A Windsor Newfoundland

Near Windsor, a servant was saved from drowning by a Newfoundland, who seized him by the collar of his coat, when he was exhausted. A Newfoundland is buried in the grounds of Windsor Castle, having rescued a man from drowning, but it is not known whether the two dogs are one and the same.

148

A Worcester Newfoundland

In the city of Worcester, one of the principal streets leads by a gentle declivity to the river Severn. One day, a child, in crossing the street, fell down in the middle of it, and a horse and cart, which were descending the hill, would have passed over it, had not a Newfoundland dog rushed to the rescue of the child, caught it up in his mouth, and conveyed it safely to the foot pavement.

Taken from "Anecdotes of Dogs" by Edward Jesse

Newfoundlands save the St Bernard

It is not generally known that importations of Newfoundland blood saved the famous Hospice Dogs of St Bernard from almost certain extinction. The Swiss dogs were seriously weakened by disease, and possibly the effects of too much in-breeding, when Newfoundlands were brought in to strengthen them in about 1831 and again in around 1856. Prior to this time, the St. Bernard had been almost exclusively a short-coated dog, but after the Newfoundland crosses, the longer coats known today became common.

A Rescue at Portsmouth

A gentleman bathing in the sea at Portsmouth, was in the greatest danger of being drowned. Assistance was loudly called for, but no boat was ready, and though many persons were looking on, no one could be found to go to his help. In this predicament, a Newfoundland dog rushed into the sea and conveyed the gentleman safely to land. He afterwards purchased the dog for a large sum, treated him as long as he lived with gratitude and kindness, and had the following words worked on his tablecloths and napkins: "Virum Extuli Mari."

Taken from "Anecdotes of Dogs" by Edward Jesse

"The Distinguished Member"

The original Distinguished Member of the Humane Society was a stray dog called Bob. Traditionally, the dog had twice been ship-wrecked with his owner. On the first occasion, he brought his master safely to shore, after a two mile swim from the ship-wreck. After the second sinking, he failed to rescue his owner and made his way to land on his own.

Bob arrived in London and made his home in dock-land. There, he gained a reputation for life-saving and the Humane Society decided to adopt him and award him their gold medal. He was officially credited with twenty-three rescues in his fourteen years of service with the Society, but there may well have been others which were not recorded. Bob must have reached a good age for a Newfoundland, since he must have been at least fifteen at the time of his death.

Archdeacon Wix's Newfoundland

I am indebted to the late, amiable Lord Stowell for the following anecdote, which has since been verified by Mr Henry Wix, brother of the Archdeacon.

A Newfoundland dog, belonging to Archdeacon Wix, which had never quitted the island, was brought over to London by him in January 1834, and when he and his family landed at Blackwell the dog was left on board the vessel. A few days afterwards the Archdeacon went from the Borough side of the Thames in a boat to the vessel, which was then in St. Katherine's Dock, to see about his luggage, but did not intend at that time to take the dog from the ship; however, on his leaving the vessel the dog succeeded in extricating himself from his confinement, jumped overboard, and swam after the boat across the Thames, followed his master into a counting-house on Gun-shot Wharf, Tooley Street and then over London Bridge and through the City to St Bartholomew's Hospital. The dog was shut within the square whilst the Archdeacon went into his father's house, and he then followed him on his way to Russell Square, but strayed somewhere in Holborn; and as several gentlemen had stopped to admire him in the street, saying he was worth a great deal of money, the Archdeacon concluded that some dog-stealer had enticed him away. He however wrote to the captain of the ship to mention his loss, and made enquiries on the following morning at St. Bartholomew's Hospital, when he learnt that the dog had come to the gates late in the evening, and howled most piteously for admission, but was driven away. Two days afterwards, the captain of the vessel waited on the Archdeacon with the dog, who had not only found his way back to the water's edge, on the Borough side, but what is more surprising, swam across the Thames, where no scent could have directed him, and found out the vessel in St. Katherine's Dock.

This sagacious and affectionate creature had, previously to his leaving Newfoundland, saved his master's life by directing his way home when lost in a snowstorm many miles from any shelter.

The dog was presented to the Archdeacon's uncle, Thomas Poynder, Esq., of Clapham Common, in whose possession it continued until his death.

Taken from "Anecdotes of Dogs" by Edward Jesse

The above story bears a curious resemblance to that of Mr Poynder's dog. Both are given, so that the reader may make up his own mind about their veracity.

A Newfoundland gives a Swimming-lesson

A Newfoundland became so disgusted at a small spaniel that would not swim out to a nearby boat, that the Newfoundland seized the spaniel by the scruff of the neck, and proceeded to give him a swimming lesson.

Taken from "Dogs, their History and Development" by Edward C. Ash

The Eslington Newfoundland

Thomas Bewick's famous woodcut was originally drawn at Eslington, in Northumberland. The estate belonged to Mr Liddell, eldest son of Lord Ravensworth. In addition to the dog, the woodcut contains four little human figures, crossing a bridge in the background. Three of the people were friends of Bewick's; Mr Preston, a printer of Newcastle, Mr Vint of Whittingham and Mr Bell, who was Mr Liddell's house-steward. The fourth little figure is Bewick himself. The initials of the four are included at the base of the woodcut.

A Newfoundland is carried away by a play

On January 28th 1858, a performance was given of the melodrama "Jessie Vere" at a Woolwich theatre. Among the audience was the chief engineer of HMS Buffalo, who was accompanied by his Newfoundland bitch. In the middle of an exciting kidnapping scene, the dog leapt onto the stage and attempted to rescue the heroine.

HMS Bellona

HMS Bellona had a Newfoundland on board, which kept the deck throughout the Battle of Copenhagen.

Roman Dogs

The Romans appear to have had a life-saving dog. In the museum at Naples there is an antique bronze, discovered amongst the ruins of Herculaneum, which represents two large dogs dragging from the sea some apparently drowned persons.

Taken from "Anecdotes of Dogs" by Edward Jesse

A Newfoundland in Siam

"And there was our own true Bessy, — a Newfoundland, great and good — discreet, reposeful, dignified, fastidious, not to be cajoled into confidences and familiarities with strange dogs, whether official or professional. Very human was her gentle countenance, and very loyal, I doubt not, her sense of responsibility, as she followed anxiously my boy and me, interpreting with the heart the thoughts she read in our faces, and responding with her sympathetic eyes."

Taken from "The English Governess at the Siamese Court" by Mrs Leonowens

Mrs Leonowens was the original Anna of the musical play
"The King and I".

The "Daily News" prize

The London "Daily News" gave a prize to a Newfoundland dog for having saved from drowning in a river a boy called Willie Frampton, and other meritorious feats.

"Mungo"

Mungo, bred in the Westerland Kennels of the Hon. Harold Macpherson, became the mascot and a crew-member of the bomber "Subconscious", in the American Air-Force, during the Second World War. He was fitted out with his own oxygen mask and parachute and went on a number of bombing flights. When the crew were posted to Britain, Mungo was in difficulties, because of quarantine restrictions. He was kept aboard the aeroplane during daylight hours and only allowed out for exercise after dark. "All cats are grey in the dark," and blacked-out London was not the best place in which to exercise a black Newfoundland. Mungo was lost, the authorities picked him up and he was placed in quarantine. By a strange coincidence, his fellow crew-members suffered a similar fate. On their very next flight over Bremen, they were shot down, and found themselves prisoners of war. Lt. Nick Robeson, who had first seen Mungo in Newfoundland and adopted him, wrote to Mr Macpherson from Germany and asked him to try and do something for the dog. After a struggle with the authorities, Mungo was shipped home to Kansas and was there to welcome Lt. Robeson when he was released from prison camp.

Taken from "This is the Newfoundland" by Mrs M K Drury

A Rescue at Eling

A Newfoundland rescued a young man from drowning in the river Test, some time towards the beginning of the 19th Century. The man, believed to be the vicar of St Mary's Church, Eling, was swimming from a bathing-machine which was situated at the end of the vicarage grounds, on the banks of the river. He found himself in difficulties and the dog, which was completely unknown to him, dived into the river and brought him safely ashore. The young man was so grateful to the dog that he attempted to buy him, but the owner refused to part with the dog. So instead, a stone statue was erected near the spot where the rescue took place.

Sadly, the Eling Vicarage is no more. Flats have been built in the old house and a bungalow stands where the statue once had pride of place. However, it is believed that descendants of the man who was rescued now have the stone dog and that it stands in the grounds of a house in Kent.

From details kindly supplied by Mrs Brinkley & Lt. Col. Robinson

Some Famous Owners

Captain Cook, Sir Walter Scott, Byron, Boswell, Dickens, Landseer, Richard Wagner, James Barrie, Robert Frost, Dimitri Rostrapovich and Arthur Koestler.

Since the 18th Century, Newfoundlands have had Royal connections. King George III owned one. Queen Victoria owned more than one and her husband Prince Albert owned Cato, which was successfully exhibited for a time. The Duke and Duchess of York, later King George V and Queen Mary, were presented with a Newfoundland when they visited the island in 1901. The dog was later to become a great favourite with their family.

Linda to the Rescue

In 1962, Mr and Mrs Henry acquired a donkey, complete with harness and a little cart. Soon afterwards, Mrs Henry harnessed the donkey, and placed her little son in the cart. He was delighted when the reins were given him to hold, while Mrs Henry started to climb into the cart. Suddenly the donkey took fright and bolted, causing Mrs Henry to lose her balance and fall. Away he went down the lane. His owner ran in pursuit but was soon exhausted.

Meanwhile, Storytime Linda, then nearly five years old, sized up the situation and gave chase. She caught up with the donkey and was seen to make several unsuccessful attempts to grab the reins, which were flying about as the donkey galloped along. Linda then decided other measures were necessary and she sprang at the donkey and forced it into the hedge, bringing it to a halt.

When Mrs Henry caught up with them, she found her child unhurt and quite unaware that his life had probably been saved by the dog.

This story was originally written by Mr W Williams in 1966

Lucky Lucy of Shermead, owned by Mr and Mrs Adey   **photo Vernon Brooke**

Attimore Libra, owned by Mrs Ward   **photo Diane Pearce**

Ch. Esmeduna's Old Chum of Mine JW, owned by Miss Crackle
photo Diane Pearce

Esmeduna's Happy Result of Orovales JW,
owned by Miss Yeoward.
photo Fall

The Landseer Newfoundland 'Dick'

CHAPTER THIRTEEN

The Landseer Newfoundland

For as long as the Newfoundland has been recognised as a distinct breed, there has been speculation about the differences between the black and the white-and-coloured varieties. Both are undoubtedly Newfoundlands, with the same basic characteristics, but there are some interesting differences. The blacks tend to be more heavily-built and to have placid temperaments. Their coats are often thicker and longer, though there are· occasional exceptions. Their heads often owe more to their distant mastiff ancestors than the Landseers'.

The Landseer tends to be a rangier dog and often has a livelier character, though he retains all the traditional magnanimity of the breed. His coat is less profuse than the black dog's, and many early specimens of the variety had curly hair.

A hundred years ago, the differences were more marked, mainly due to a reluctance by breeders to interbreed the blacks and Landseers. Two world wars, and a consequent shortage of blood-lines, have forced breeders to mix the colours, with beneficial results in terms of greater uniformity of type.

It has been suggested that an importation of Large White Estate Dogs (or Butcher's Dogs) to the main part of Newfoundland may have been responsible for the development of the Landseer. There is very little evidence that the Estate Dog ever existed as a recognised breed and it seems more probable that these dogs were early Pyreneans or Mastiffs. When considering the latter, it should be remembered that white was a relatively common mastiff colour years ago, although it is now unacceptable to modern breeders. Velasquez included a black-and-white mastiff in his painting of Prince Baldassare Carlo. The dog's head is much like a present-day New-foundland's. Just over a hundred years later, in 1780, Sawry Gilpin painted the Duke of Hamilton's Mastiff, and showed him to be a short-haired dog with perfect "Landseer" markings.

The curly coats of some early Landseers suggest that the Large Rough Water Dog may have played a **part in** their evolution. Illustrations of these dogs show them to have been predominantly white, though Gervase Markham wrote that they could by of any colour.

It seems very likely that both spaniels and sheepdogs may be included in the Landseer background. Spaniels would have been essential to early settlers, if they were to hunt for food. Sheepdogs were certainly taken to Newfoundland by immigrants who tried to establish sheep farms there.

Given the basic recipe; isolation and the particular demands of in-dividual communities ensured the development of different types of New-foundland, although they all retained certain common characteristics, such as their love of working in the water and their excellent disposition. Smaller, black dogs suited the seagoing people of the South-western coast and off-shore islands, while the Landseers developed further North and inland.

When referring to colours, it is probably more accurate to define the black dogs as whole-coloured, since bronze, grey and black-and-tan were all seen from time to time. Similarly, the Landseers were not solely white-and-black. Rawdon B. Lee, writing in "Modern Dogs" made reference to Newfoundlands at the end of the 18th Century, as "Large, rough-coated, curly-haired, liver-and-white dogs." Since then, human tastes and fads have played their part. At the start of importation into Europe, more or less equal numbers of each variety were brought over. As the whole-coloured dogs became the preference of shooting men, so the Landseers became the favourites of those who wished to keep them as pets. The beauty of their markings became very important. Sir Edwin Landseer certainly brought their popularity to a peak with his portrait of "The Dis-tinguished Member of the Humane Society", and for a short time the whole-coloured dogs suffered a partial eclipse. However, by the time formal records were being kept by the Kennel Club, registrations seem to have been balanced in their favour.

By 1899, T E Mansfield wrote, "The Landseers have not made such progress as the blacks, for the simple reason that breeders of this variety will not go back to the black dogs to improve the coat and type of their black-and-whites . . . . The majority of the dogs in this division are bad in coat, which often resembles the back of a Shropshire sheep; they generally fall off in their hindquarters, being tucked up in the loin and leggy, and lack quality and type." Nevertheless, some lovely dogs were being bred at this time, Ch.Prince of Norfolk and his son Ch.Prince of Suffolk among them.

Since World War I, the white-and-black dogs have had a lean time. Numbers of suitable breeding animals were reduced almost to nil and efforts to increase the stock were hampered by the fact that most of the leading kennels of that era preferred the black variety. Miss Reid's Daventry kennel was an outstanding exception.

At the present time, the white-and-black dogs are making something of a come-back, largely due to the efforts of breeders like Mrs Roberts, Mrs Handley, Miss Morrison, Mr Blyth and Mr Frost. They have been helped by a number of imported dogs and bitches from Europe and America, which have fortunately blended well together, and with existing British lines, to produce some lovely animals. Today's Landseer in no way resembles Mr Mansfield's despised "Shropshire sheep".

As long as leading breeders continue to show a preference for dogs of one colour, to the exclusion of the other, there will be minor differences between them. Even so, they are all Newfoundlands, with the same essential breed characteristics, and any attempt to divide them should be strongly resisted. Present-day breeders are probably closer to uniformity between the two varieties than ever before. Separation would be retrograde and damaging.

Newfoundland Dog by Thomas Bewick

CHAPTER FOURTEEN

THE NEWFOUNDLAND CLUB

by

Miss J M DAVIES

The Newfoundland Club was the first club for the breed to be established. It was founded in 1886, when Mr William van Oppen, Mr van Weede, Mr Gillingham, Mr J B Bailey and others decided on its formation. It is one of the oldest specialist breed clubs in existence. At the time of the club's founding it was common for many clubs to be formed earlier than their original date of registration with the Kennel Club, and the Newfoundland Club did not register until 1891, when Mr E Nichols made the necessary application.

The first intention of the founder members was, "To establish the standard and type for the breed now acknowledged by Newfoundland Clubs throughout the world." An aim which has proved eminently successful.

Over the years, the Club's rules have been revised. The first record of the rules is 1902, though there is only a note to the effect that the revised rules were passed, without any mention of the ammendments. In 1903 it was decided that Officers, Committee and Judges should be elected triennially, instead of annually. The return to annual elections of officers and one-third of the Committee took place in 1931, though in the intermediary period (1924) new rules and bye-laws were adopted. Up to 1971 the office of President and Chairman were combined, but in that year it was decided to separate them. The President is now triennially elected by members at the Annual General Meeting. The Chairman is elected annually by and from the Committee, which numbers ten.

In the immediate post-war years, when the breed was at a very low ebb, the office of Honorary Treasurer and Honorary Secretary were combined in the person of our current President Mrs Charles Roberts. In 1954, membership had increased to such an extent that it was agreed to return to having two officers, and Mrs Vernon Handley became Treasurer, remaining in that position until 1976, with Mrs Roberts continuing as Secretary, until the election of the present writer in 1967.

The system of appointing judges prior to 1911 is not clear, but there is mention in the minutes that the then President gave notice, "That the rule confining the number of judges at eight shall stand without defining a number." It was also proposed that judges travelling a distance should have expenses within reasonable limits paid by the Club, with the Committee subsequently being given discretionary powers in this respect.

Naze Blaze, with her owner Harry Pettit, who designed the Club letter-head. Blaze was bred by Mr Blyth and was the first Landseer to be whelped in Britain after the Second World War

At the present time Show Societies bear the cost of judge's fees and travelling expenses. There is also no limit to the number of names on a club's judging list, though the Kennel Club does advise the inclusion of a percentage of all-rounders to specialists. The judging list is divided into three sections, A, B and C. List "A" comprises persons approved by the Kennel Club to award Challenge Certificates. The "B" list comprises persons considered qualified to award Certificates and who the Club is prepared to support if invited to award certificates in the breed. Those persons on the "C" list are considered qualified to judge.

The allocation of Certificates has changed over the years. Prior to 1920, some show societies offered one set each for the blacks and white-and-blacks. When registrations were at a very low level, Challenge Certificates were withheld altogether. This resulted in few champions being made up in the years following the Second War.

From 1911 until after the First World War there is a gap in the Club records and it appears to have been 1921 before another Club meeting was held. This was attended by both the late Mr H Keeling (uncle of Miss Mollie Crump) and Mr W Morgan, both of whom had a great influence in the breed and on Club affairs.

In 1922, the Club was invited to become a member of "The Newfoundland Club of the Continent", but it was decided to decline the invitation because of the, "Small membership and the existence of similar blood in dogs belonging to both clubs." Subsequently, in 1927, the Kennel Club issued a directive, which has to be included in the rules of all breed clubs, that such clubs shall not join any federation or societies of clubs.

By 1925, the Honorary Secretary of that time, Lt-Col. Wetwan, in his annual report, said that, "After a period of more or less suspended animation in which no meetings were held and very few records were kept, the Club awoke to a newness of life early in 1924."

So commenced a period of stabilisation. The Club continued on an even tenor, supporting classes at shows with guarantees, special prizes, etc., and in turn being upheld by dedicated breeders who, in spite of the high mortality among adult and young dogs prevalent in the Twenties, gained steady recognition for the breed.

Then came the Second World War, with disastrous results for the Newfoundland, and nearly all that had gone before was brought to nought. A practically "dead" period ensued, during which Mrs Roberts, who had been elected Honorary Secretary in 1935, personally paid the Maintenance Fee to the Kennel Club, thus ensuring unbroken registration for ninety years.

It was November 1947 before the surviving stalwarts of the breed were to meet again, electing a Committee which included Mr and Mrs Handley, who had joined the Club in 1932. A mammoth task confronted these few: the resurrection of a badly depleted breed and Club. Nothing daunted, they slowly and methodically set to work, and succeeded by selfless effort in re-establishing the breed. At the outset of their struggle, there were ten Newfoundlands in Britain, some of which were not in their first youth. The story of their fight for survival is traced elsewhere.

Through the good offices and generosity in lean times of its supporters, with donations in cash and kind, the Club has remained financially solvent.

Breed fanciers have always been generous with gifts of silver and the Club is well-endowed with trophies. Pride of place must surely go to the four Challenge Cups, one for each sex in blacks and Landseers. To read the inscriptions on the plinths is to turn the pages of a book of living history. 1898 is the first date on the black dog cup, 1895 on the bitch one. No date is given for the first winner of the Black-and-White dog cup, but the second one was in 1894. The dates for the Black-and-White bitch cup start in 1897. The cups appear to have been on offer at various shows, and sometimes more than once in the same year. Among the shows were, Crufts, Crystal Palace, the Kennel Club Show, Earl's Court, Cardiff, Alexandra Palace and Manchester. As the dates when these cups were donated were prior to the commencement of known records, the donors and the cost must remain unknown. However, contemporary show reports in canine journals suggest that they were originally known as the Fifty Guinea Cups. Their present-day value must be greatly in excess of this and

The Club Challenge Cups

we must always remain grateful to those who fashioned such beautiful trophies and to those who donated them. There is little that compares with the pride in being custodian of one for a year, if you are fortunate enough to win one.

Another trophy whose origins are lost in the mist of time is the Edwards Shield. Originally it was on offer for the best team, and was competed for in Ireland. It is currently offered for the best brace, as team classes are not scheduled.

Gold and Silver medals, and bronze statuettes are among the pre-war trophies which could be won outright, and are still the proud possessions of the doyens of the breed.

The Club lapel badge was introduced in 1938 and depicts the head of Am.Ch.Harlingen Neptune. Unfortunately, Messrs Elkington of Birmingham were bombed during the war and all the dies were destroyed. Only the lapel badge and statuette were replaced. In the 1960's a car badge was introduced. Outright wins are commemorated nowadays by ashtrays or tiles or glasses with Newfoundland Club designs on them.

Over the years the Club has had three different letter-heads. The first in

1935 incorporated an advertisement for Spillers dog foods. The second, first printed in 1953, was decorated with Harlingen Neptune's head. The third, which is the present-day format, was designed free by the late Mr Harry Pettitt in the Club colours agreed at the time of black-and-white and sea-green. Mr David Blyth very generously donated the cost of making the block.

The first recorded Newfoundland water trials appear to have been held at Maidstone in 1876. Since then, they have been held at intervals throughout the Club's history, but they did not become a regular annual event until 1965. Now, thanks to Mrs Juliet Gibson's efforts and enthusiasm in finding a venue and interesting fellow breed enthusiasts, the Club holds trials each year, which include a match meeting and basic obedience competition. There is also a carting display and contest.

The first Club Newsletter was brought out in 1966 by the present writer who edited it for a year, until she became Secretary and handed it over to Mrs Muriel Shearwood. Mrs Shearwood continued to produce the Newsletter until 1972, when Mr and Mrs Symes took over.

During the Newsletter's ten years of life it has altered considerably. More sophisticated methods of production have meant that photographs can now be included, and the quality of the print and the size of the publication have been improved. Throughout its existence it has tried to maintain a high standard, in spite of rising costs. It is now published quarterly, and as a means of bringing our scattered members into closer contact, it is invaluable. Long may it continue to flourish.

The breed itself is probably stronger, in terms of over-all quality, than it has ever been and the present generation of breeders must ensure that it remains so. They have a responsibility to see that the achievements of the past are not only maintained, but improved upon. They have, largely thanks to the efforts of a dedicated few in the post-war years, a wider choice of blood-lines to work with than at any other time since the turn of the century. However, they must never forget in their quest for excellence that, for every one or two show-standard puppies born in a litter, there may be six or eight others who simply need loving homes. In a world which seems to grow steadily poorer and hungrier, the demand for large pets is decreasing. It is therefore up to every breeder to think carefully before embarking on a litter. In this way, standards may be upheld, without endangering the welfare of our lovely Newfoundlands.

Presidents of the Newfoundland Club (Combining the office of Chairman up to 1974)

Mr A van Weede
Mr J.J. Cooper
Mr Lindsay
Mrs Wetwan
Mr J.J. Horsfield
Mr D. Brand
Mr G. Bland
Lt-Col J.Reid-Kerr
Mr H.McCann
Miss Reid

Mr H.Steggles
Mr W. H. Morgan
Mr Shaw
Mr D.Blyth
Mr V.Handley
Mr C.Roberts
Mrs Pat Handley
Mr Hamilton-Gould
Mrs K.Rowsell
Mrs C.Roberts (elected in 1974, when
    Mr Handley became Chairman)

Honorary Secretaries
Mr W.Gillingham
Mr L.Hodge
Mr W.H.Morgan
Mr D.Brand
Lt-Col Wetwan
Mrs C. Roberts
Miss J.M.Davies

Honorary Treasurers
Mr van Oppen
Capt. J.H.Bailey
Mr H. Keeling
Mr Owen Thomas
Mrs C. Roberts (combined with Hon. Secretary)
Mrs C. Handley
Mrs J. Warren

Ch. Stormsail Matterhorn JW, owned by Mr and Mrs Oriani

photo Diane Pearce

*Ch. Stormsail Wetterhorn JW, owned
by Mr and Mrs Oriani*

photo Diane Pearce

LANDSEER - NEWFOUNDLAND . CH. KETTERING WONDER². LADY TOLLEMACHE OWNER .

THE LARGE ROUGH WATER-DOG

"The behaviour of a Newfoundland Dog should be such that a child could lead him on a silken thread."

from The Kennel Encyclopaedia by F.T.Barton

ERRATA:

page 12 — "Thames" should read Thame
page 21 — "Mr Gibson" should read Mrs Gibson
plate following page 41 — caption should read "Ch. Siki".
page 112 — caption of 2nd and 3rd drawings should be reversed

Appendix I

A list of kennel names, including a small number of overseas ones which have played a significant part in British pedigrees.

Abbylake	Mr and Mrs L. George
Attimore	Mrs E. M. H. Denham
Avalons	Mr A. G. P. van Zijl (Holland)
Bacalieu	Mrs Bowers
Bachalaos	Mr and Mrs J. B. Dick-Cleland
Barlight	Mr and Mrs G. Symes
Barribals	Mr Tempel (Holland)
Bluespring	Mrs J. Masters
Bonnybay	Mr and Mrs D. Lucas
Brookford	Mr and Mrs Gunn
Bulwell	Mr H. E. Steggles
Cabstar	Mr B. D. Kitson
Caladh	Mrs R. E. Blackman
Caledon	Mr E. Gianini
Capespear	Miss Read
Carolsown	Mrs D. S. Cooper
Charlesworth	Mrs and Miss Greenall
Clywoods	Mr and Mrs C. Woods
Cobblecove	Mr P. Spicer
Colmer	Mr N. Kennard
Daventry	Miss Reid
Deanfield	Mr and Mrs W. Springthorpe
Dryads	Mr and Mrs Maynard K. Drury (USA)
Eaglebay	Mr and Mrs C. Gladwin
Ebony Haze (previously Naze)	Mr D. Blyth
Esmeduna	Mr and Mrs C. Whittaker
Fairwater	Mrs V. Handley
Gerahmeen	Mr and Mrs A. Shearwood
Gleborchd	Lt-Col Reid-Kerr
Greenayre	Mrs Braid
Hambledown	Mr and Mrs G. Pratt
Harlingen	Mrs Charles Roberts
Harmonattan	Mr and Mrs Saloranta (Finland)
Harratons	Messrs Frost & Bell
Highfoo	Mr and Mrs W. L. Winston
Isambard	Mrs Clarke
Karazan	Mrs P. Colgan
Kingfishereach	Mrs Withal
Knole	Lord Sackville
Lantivet	Mr and Mrs D. Sharpe
Laphroaig	Mrs K. Gibson
Little Bear	Mr and Mrs V. A. Chern (USA)
Littlecreek	Mr and Mrs F. Cassidy
Mapleopal	Mr and Mrs M. Ludlow
Marun	Mrs Ruskeala (Finland)
Merikarhun	Mr J. Salminen (Finland)
Middleham	Miss Topham
Midway	Mr and Mrs F. Stubbart (USA)
Mishow	Mr and Mrs B. Phillips
Nasealga	Mrs J. Stewart

Naze (see Ebony Haze)
Netherwood.. Miss Dent
Norepoint................................... Mr and Mrs C. Shaw
Orovales.. Miss M. Yeoward
Perryhow.. Mrs Bennett
Plaisance.. Mr T. McKenna
Ragtime.. Mr G. Alcock
Rathpeacon .... Mr and Mrs P. Gale (Ireland)
Rhenus.. Mrs K. Rowsell
Roydsrook .... Mr and Mrs D. Wilson
Sealcove... Mrs L. M. Withey
Seaward... Mrs E. Ayres (USA)
Shelton.......................... Mrs Nicholas (later Mrs Wetwan)
Shermead .... Mr and Mrs J. Adey
Sigroc.. Miss J. M. Davies
Sparry.. Mrs M. Aberdeen
Starbeck.......................... Miss Goodall (the prefix "Gipsy" was used)
Stormsail................................... Mr and Mrs P. Oriani
Storytime....................................... Mrs B. Henry
Suisseberne..................................... Mrs L. Mason
Sukiln .... Miss E. Osmond
Suleskerry....................................... Miss I. Morrison
Tarnhill..................................... Mr and Mrs Taylor
Tonsarne................................. Mr and Mrs N. Teasdale
Uskrail .... Miss V. Chadwick
van de Negerhut .... Mr and Mrs J. Pieterse (Holland)
       (this kennel name sometimes appears translated as "Uncle Tom's Cabin")
Verduron..................................... Mrs G. Shapland
Wanitopa....................................... Mrs J. Gibson
Waseeka .... Mrs E. Davieson-Power (USA)
Whitehouse..................................... Mrs J. Hobson
Witchazel..................................... Miss Herdsman
Wildfields..................................... Mr Roberts

Insert on page 163

Littlegrange .... Mrs. J. Warren

Appendix II

A List of All Known British or British-Bred Champions and Junior Warrant Holders

While this list is as accurate as possible, it is only as correct as the records themselves. Early breeders frequently changed dogs' names or used the same name for two or three dogs in the same kennel. Popular names like Nep, Nelson, Nell, Leo, Prince and The Black Prince often recur. Some dogs have been listed as champions in old pedigrees when they were nothing of the kind, while others should have been and were not. Where possible, the colours of the dogs have been given.

Achates of Fairwater—Black dog (1960)
Owned/Bred: Mrs C. Handley
Patriot of Witchazel x Naze Snowdrop
Achilles of Fairwater—Black dog (1957)
Patriot of Witchazel x Naze Snowdrop
Owned: Mr P. Gale/Bred: Mrs C. Handley
Admiral Drake—White/Black dog (1882)
Pedigree unknown
Owned: Mrs. E. Nichols
Alderman—Dog (1883)
Ch. Joe Saddler x Lady-in-Waiting
Owned: Mr Mansfield/Bred: Mr H. R. Farquharson, MP
Alliance—Dog (1884)
Ch. Gunville x Ch. Sybil
Owned: J. Green/Bred, Mr Mansfield
Armada—Bitch
Bred: Mr Mansfield
Athol Roy—White/Black dog (1899)
Pompi (unregistered) x Fell's Bute (unregistered)
Attimore Aquarius—Black bitch (1969)
Ch. Lord Hercules of Fairwater x Wanitopa Mermaid
Owned/Bred: Mrs E. Denham
Attimore Minches—Black bitch (1971)
Ch. Lord Hercules of Fairwater x Wanitopa Mermaid
Owned: Mrs Randall/Bred: Mrs E. Denham
Attimore Royal Sovereign—Black dog (1973)
Avalons Ikaros of Littlegrange x Wanitopa Mermaid
Owned: Mr & Mrs Dorman/Bred: Mrs E. Denham
Bachalaos Bright Water of Stormsail—Black bitch (1972)
Samson of Fairwater x Attimore Virgo
Owned: Mr & Mrs Oriani/Bred: Mr & Mrs Dick-Cleland
Barlight Buccaneer of Littlecreek—Black dog (1973)
Ch. Capt. Starlight of Littlegrange x Ch. Seashell of Littlecreek
Owned: Mr F. Cassidy/Bred: Mr & Mrs Symes
Can. Ch. Baron—Black dog (1928)
Ch. Siki x Harlingen Topsy
Owned: Mr Oliver/Bred: Mrs C. Roberts
Bear I Do Love You of Esmeduna—Black dog (1968)
Avalons Ikaros of Littlegrange x Lace and Dimity of Esmeduna
Owned/Bred: Mr & Mrs C. Whittaker

Beechgrove Princess—Bitch (1897)
Bred from a bitch named Duchess (unregistered). No other details known

Binambi's Daughter—Bitch (C1900)
Owned: W. A. Goodwin

Bismark—Dog. No other details known

Black and White—White/Black dog (1924)
Ch. Captain Courageous x Maori Girl
Owned: Mr Morgan/Bred: Mr Bland

Black and White Prince—White/Black dog (1885)
Peter the Great x Dingley's Daisy
Owned: Mrs Chapman/Bred: Mr Dingley

Black Bess—Black bitch (1924)
Ch. Siki x Ch. Waterwitch
Owned: Lt-Col Reid-Kerr/Bred: Mr Brand

Black Jet of Littlegrange—Black dog (1962)
Sailorboy of Verduron x Miranda of Verduron
Owned/Bred: Mrs J. Warren

The Black Prince—Black dog (1883)
Ch. Nelson I x Jennie
Owned: Mrs Mansfield or Mr Bennett/Bred: Mr Meacock

Eng. & Aus Ch. Bonnybay Jasmine—Black bitch (1961)
Ch. Achates of Fairwater x Ch. Bonnybay Nona of Sparry
Owned: Mrs J. Gibson/Bred: Mr & Mrs Lucas

Bonnybay Mister Barrel—Black dog (1961)
Ch. Achates of Fairwater x Ch. Bonnybay Nona of Sparry
Owned/Bred: Mr & Mrs D. Lucas

Bonnybay Musette of Sparry—White/Black bitch (1959)
Sparry's King of Hearts — Sparry's Amphitrite of Fairwater
Owned: Mr & Mrs Lucas/Bred: Mrs Aberdeen

Bonnybay Nona of Sparry—Black bitch (1958)
Ch. Sea Lord of Sparry x Sea-Drift of Sparry
Owned: Mr & Mrs D. Lucas/Bred: Mrs Aberdeen

Boodles Esq—Black dog (1888)
Ch. Courtier x Baroness
Owned: Mrs Mansfield

Bowden Perfection—Black dog (1900)
Ch. King Stuart x Seaweed
Owned: Mr Horsfield/Bred: Mr J. J. Cooper

Brave Michael—Black dog (1928)
Ch. Siki x Una of Chinnor
Owned: Miss V. H. Deane/Bred: E. Heden-Copus

Bridgford Gem—Bitch (1910). No other details known
x Lady Melbourne

Am. Ch. Bulwell Aero Flame—Black bitch (C1929)
Ch. Brave Michael x The Gift

Canonbury Rover—White/Black dog (1896)
Earl of Canonbury x Nell (unregistered)

Cantisfield Velvet—Black bitch
Ch. Boddles Esq x Lady Mayoress

Captain Courageous—Black dog (1921)
Cedric from Galphay x Galphay Blackberry
Owned: Miss Herdsman/Bred: Mrs Melville-White

Captain Starlight of Littlegrange—Black dog (1970)
Ch. Black Jet of Littlegrange x Cottleston Pie of Esmeduna
Owned: Mrs J. Warren/Bred: Mr C. Whittaker

Cascar Merikoira—Black dog (1969)
Ch. Sigroc King Neptune x Esmeduna's Joyous Roundelay
Owned: Mrs S. Sharpe/Bred: Mr Sandford

Cherry of Littlegrange—Black bitch (1962)
Sailorboy of Verduron x Miranda of Verduron
Owned/Bred: Mrs J. Warren

Chieftain Bill—Black dog (1934)
Uz x Harlingen Lou
Owned: Mr W. R. Squires/Bred: Mrs C. Handley

Claverhouse II—Dog (1893)
x Milne's Topsy

Clywoods Worthy Boy—Black dog (1971)
Avalon's Ikaros of Littlegrange x A Maiden Tender of Esmeduna
Owned: Mr C. Corderoy/Bred: Mr & Mrs C. Woods

Coastguard—Dog
Bred: Mr Mansfield

Commander

Courtier—Black dog (1881)
Ch. Nelson x Jennie
Owned: Mr H. R. Farquharson, MP/Bred: E. Nichols

Daisy Queen—Black bitch (1906)
Ch. Shelton Viking x Molly Bawn
Owned: E. Parkinson/Bred: H. W. Yates

Daventry Brigantine—Black bitch (1935)
Daventry Mariner x Daventry Siren
Owned: Miss Topham/Bred: Miss Reid

Dick—White/Black dog (1871)
Vass's Neptune x Evan's Nell
Owned/Bred: Mr R. Evans

Donald—Black dog (1928)
Leo x Gipsy (unregistered)

Dondo—White/Black dog (1902)
Lord Methuen x Jester or Gester
Owned: Mr J. J. Horsfield

Donovan II—White/Black dog (1892)
Royal Bruce x England's Pride

Drift of Littlecreek—Black bitch (1962)
Ch. Sea Urchin of Sparry x Littlecreek's Sea Imp of Perryhow
Owned/Bred: Mr. F. Cassidy

Duke of Stoke
Owned: Mrs H. Hodgson

Am. Ch. Eaglebay Domino—White/Black dog (1961)
Ch. Achates of Fairwater x Jane of Rhenus
Owned: Mrs I. Clarke/Bred: Mr & Mrs Gladwin

Echo—Black dog (C1933)
Owned: Mr Lane

Esmeduna's Annalisa of Sigroc—Black bitch (1970)
Ch. Black Jet of Littlegrange x Cottleston Pie of Esmeduna
Owned: Miss J. Davies/Bred: Mr. C. Whittaker

Esmeduna's Old Chum of Mine (JW)—Black dog (1974)
Ch. Sigroc King Neptune x Ch. I'm Dimpy Too of Esmeduna
Owned: Mrs & Miss Crackle/Bred: Mr C. Whittaker

Faithful of Littlegrange—Black bitch (1962)
Sailorboy of Verduron x Miranda of Verduron
Owned: Miss J. Davies/Bred: Mrs J. Warren

Fearless Foundation—White/Black dog (1909)
Alpha x Fearless Emblem
Owned: Mrs Lindsay/Bred: Mr Fearn

Ferrol Lou—Black bitch (1924)
Ch. Captain Courageous x Maori Girl

Ferrol Neptune—Black dog (1919)
Ch. Gipsy Boy x Galphay Jess
Owned: Mr J. J. Horsfield/Bred: Mrs Bland

Fisher Maid—Black bitch (1915)
Silent Knight x Molly
Owned: Mr Brand

Friendly Drelb of Esmeduna—Black dog (1969)
Avalons Ikaros of Littlegrange x A Maiden Tender of Esmeduna
Owned: Mr Gentile/Bred: Mr C. Whittaker

Gannel Echo—Black dog (1926)
Ch. Siki x Harlingen Topsy
Owned: Mrs H. Cardell/Bred: Mr W. Bursey

Gentle Bear of Aston—Black dog (1971)
Ch. Laphroaig Attimore Aries x Morning Star Maiden
Owned: Mr & Mrs Harding/Bred: Mr Gianini

Gipsy Baron—Black dog (1911)
Ch. Fearless Foundation x Rita (previously Beta)
Owned: Miss Goodall/Bred: Mr Fearn

Gipsy Boy—Black dog (1914)
Ch. Gipsy Baron x Anchoria
Owned: Miss Goodall

Gipsy Duchess—Black bitch (1906)
Ch. Shelton Viking x Molly Bawn
Owned: Miss Goodall/Bred: Mr Yates

Gipsy Duke—Black dog (1906)
Ch. Shelton Viking x Molly Bawn
Owned: Miss Goodall/Bred: Mr Yates

Gipsy Peeress—Black bitch (1913)
Ch. Gipsy Duke x Mollie
Owned/Bred: Miss Goodall

Gipsy Princess—Black bitch (1899)
Ch. Wolf of Badenoch x Humber Peeress
Owned: Miss Goodall/Bred: Mr Haldenby

Gleborchd Boss—Black dog (1924)
Ch. Siki x Ch. Waterwitch
Owned: Lt-Col Reid-Kerr/Bred: Mr Brand

Grand Master—Dog (1903)
Ch. Humber Jumbo x Bessie (unregistered)
Owned: Mr C. H. Graham/Bred: Mr Wilkinson

Greenayre Dogwatch—Black dog (1972)
Avalon's Ikaros of Littlegrange x Harraton's Loustelle
Owned: Miss Totty/Bred: Mrs Braid

Gunville—Black dog (1880)
Ch. Theodore Nero x Queen of Night
Owned: Mr H. R. Farquharson, MP

Hanlon (or Hanlan)—Dog (1883)
Ch. Joe Saddler x Lady-in-Waiting
Owned/Bred: Mr H. R. Farquharson, MP

Harlingen Ace—Black dog (C1924)
Ch. Black & White x Queen of Hearts
Owned/Bred: Mrs C. Roberts

Harlingen Aphrodite of Fairwater—Black bitch (1951)
Brave Serestus x Ch. Harlingen Brigantine
Owned: Mrs V. Handley/Bred: Mrs C. Roberts

Harlingen Black Cherry—Black bitch (1951)
Brave Serestus x Ch. Harlingen Brigantine
Owned: Miss Herdsman/Bred: Mrs C. Roberts

Harlingen Brigantine—Black bitch (1949)
Waseeka's Dauntless x Harlingen Waseeka's Black Gold
Owned/Bred: Mrs C. Roberts

Harlingen Cedric— White/Black dog (1928)
Robin (unregistered) x Ferrol Lou
Owned: Mrs V. Roberts/Bred: A. C. de Moor

Harlingen Coastguard — Black dog (1949)
Waseeka's Dauntless x Harlingen Waseeka's Black Gold
Owned: Mrs C. Handley/Bred: Mrs. C. Roberts

Harlingen Drifter — Black dog (1931)
Harlingen Ace x Nance of Cobblegate
Owned: Mr W. Morgan/Bred: Mrs C. Roberts

Harlingen Earl — White/Black dog (1928)
Ch.Black and White x Harlingen Mermaid
Owned: Mr O. Thomas/Bred: Mrs C. Roberts

Am.Ch.Harlingen Jess of Waseeka — Black bitch (1925)
Ch.Siki x Queen Bess
Owned: Mrs Davieson-Power/Bred: Mrs C. Roberts

Am.Ch.Harlingen Neptune — Black dog (1926)
Ch.Siki x Ch.Queen of Hearts
Owned: Mrs E.H.Lewin/Bred: Mrs. C. Roberts

Harlingen Pirate — Black dog (1949)
Waseeka's Dauntless x Harlingen Waseeka's Black Gold
Owned: Mrs Mayhew/Bred: Mrs C. Roberts

Harlingen Sandpiper — White/Black dog (1959)
Ch.Achates of Fairwater x Harlingen Taaran-Taru
Owned: Mrs Hamilton-Gould/Bred: Mrs C. Roberts

Can.Ch.Harlingen Sea Shell — White/Black bitch (C1970)
Suleskerry Sailmaker of Fairwater x Ch. Harlingen Wanitopa Moonlight
Owned: Mr J. Jones/Bred: Mrs C. Roberts

Harlingen Wanitopa Moonlight — White/Black bitch (1965)
Suleskerry Steersman x Eng.&.Aus.Ch.Bonnybay Jasmine
Owned: Mrs C. Roberts/Bred: Mrs J. Gibson

Havelock — Dog (1895)

Hecate — Bitch (1934)
Sir Launcelot x Deborah the Prophetess
Owned/Bred: Miss Topham

Help — Black bitch (1924)
Ch.Siki x Ch.Waterwitch
Owned: Miss Herdsman/Bred: Mr Brand

Highfoo Harratons Ocean Queen — White/Black bitch (1969)
Suleskerry Sailmaker of Fairwater x Whitehouse Sea Diver
Owned: Mr W. L. Winston/Bred: Messrs Frost & Bell

SA.Ch.Highfoo Sea Urchin—Black bitch
Ch.Sigroc King Neptune x Harlingen Puffin of Highfoo
Owned: Mr & Mrs Buckley/Bred: Mr W.L. Winston

His Nibs — White/Black dog
Bruce II x Cain

Humber Jumbo — Dog (1901)
Humber Captain x Duchess of Hornsea

Humber Surprise — Bitch(1904)
Ch.Humber Jumbo x Humber Gem
Bred: Mr C.C. Haldenby

I'm Dimpy Too of Esmeduna — Black bitch (1970)
Ch.Bear I Do Love You of Esmeduna x Ch.Storytime Black Pearl of Esmeduna
Owned/Bred: Mr C. Whittaker

Am.Ch.Isambard Odin the Viking — Dog (1965)
Am.Ch.Eaglebay Domino x Storytime Tarbaby of Sparry   Bred: Mrs Clarke

Jack Tar — Dog
Owned: Mr Cameron/Bred: Mr Mansfield.

Joe Saddler — Black dog (1879)
Scamp x Duchess
Owned/Bred: Mr H.R. Farquharson, MP

Kaiserin — Bitch (1907)
x Countess Hedworth

Ken — Black dog (1899)
Ch.Donovan x Milkmaid
Owned: F. Gibbons/Bred: Mr Mansfield

Kettering Scout—Dog
Lord Byron x Bonny Lassie

Kettering Wonder — White/Black dog (1896)
Owned: Lady Tollemach

King Stuart — Black dog (1892)
Prince Jack x Annie or Queen Anne
Owned: Mr King

Lady Buller — Black bitch (1900)
Ch.King Stuart x Seaweed
Owned: Mr Critchley/Bred: Mr J.J. Cooper

Lady Ferrol — Black bitch (1922)
Ch.Gipsy Boy x Lady Mayco
Owned: Mrs McCann/Bred: Mr J.J. Horsefield

Lady Marion — Black bitch (1932)
Ch.Water Rat x Queenie of the Green
Owned/Bred: Mr H.S. Gunn

Lady Mayoress — Black bitch (1881)
Ch.Nelson II x Jennie (imported)
Owned/Bred: Mrs E. Nichols

Lady Teazle — Bitch (1884)
Ch.Nelson II x Marzeppa
Owned: Mr G. Chapman/Bred: Mrs E Nichols

Laphroaig Attimore Aries — Black dog (1969)
Ch.Lord Hercules of Fairwater x Wanitopa Mermaid
Owned: Mrs K. Gibson/Bred: Mrs E. Denham

Leo — Black dog (1872)
Windle's Don x Meg of Maldon
Owned/Bred: Mr W Coates

Lifebuoy — White/Black dog (1931)
Ch.Harlingen Cedric x Harlingen Anne
Owned/Bred: Mr W. Johnson

Lincoln Dick — White/Black dog (C1900)
Ch.Canonbury Rover x Shelton (previously Lincoln) Snowflake

Lincoln Snowflake (later Shelton Snowflake) — White/Black bitch (1895)
Ch.Pirate Chief x Lincoln Abbess
Owned: L. Hodges/Bred: Mr Eastwood

Lion — Dog (1875)
Ch.Leo x Nell
Owned: Mr S. Wildman/Bred: Mr C.W. Shaw

Littlecreeks Son of Rex — — Black dog (1962)
Ch.Sea Urchin of Sparry x Ch.Littlecreeks Sea Imp of Perryhow
Owned/Bred: Mr F. Cassidy

Littlegrange Anna — Black bitch (1972)
Ch.Capt. Starlight of Littlegrange x Your Sweet Bippy of Esmeduna
Owned: Miss Crackle/Bred: Mrs J. Warren

Longscar Jess — Black bitch (1905)
Ch.Shelton Viking x Ch.Humber Surprise
Owned: Mrs Eve/Bred: Mr Haldenby

Lonsdale — Dog (1888)

Lord Hercules of Fairwater — Black dog (1967)
Harmonattan Okay x Marun Kiva
Owned: Mrs C. Handley/Bred: Miss R. Friend

Lord Nelson — Dog (1883)
Nelson I x Thora
Owned: Mrs E. Nichols/Bred: Mr Wellacott

Lucky Lucy of Shermead — White/Black bitch (1975)
Shermead Lord Mars x Greenayre Bon Flair
Owned: Mr & Mrs Adey/Bred: Mrs Bury

Lunaire — Black bitch (1925)
Ch.Siki x Ch.Waterwitch
Owned: Lt-Col Reid-Kerr/Bred: Mr Brand

Maid of Thalassa — Black bitch (1931)
Ch.Gleborchd Boss x Ebony Lass
Owned: J.B.Dawson/Bred: H. Brown

Majestic — Black dog (1931)
Old Salt x Foam
Owned/Bred: Mr Bland

Master Jumbo — Dog (1889)
Nero x

Mayor of Bingley — Dog (1877)
Sam x Kinloch's Fly
Owned: Mr Wildman/Bred: Mr Kinloch

Meg of Galphay — Black bitch
Ch.Gipsy Duke x Tyno Queen
Owned: Mr Wildman/Bred: Mr Kinloch

Merikarhun Fay of Sigroc — Black bitch (1966)
Fin.Ch.Alderbay Attila x Merikarhun Desiré
Owned: Miss J.M. Davies/Bred: Mr J. Salminen

Mermaid — Black bitch (1928)
Ch.Siki x Seagrave Belle
Owned: Mr H.S.Gunn/Bred: Mr G. Bland

Merrie Lassie — Bitch (1895)
Ch.Merry Boy x Duchess of York

Merry Boy — White/Black dog (1891)
Ch.Black and White Prince x Canonbury Bell

Merry Maiden — Bitch (C1890)
Ch.Boodles Esq x Ch.Lady Mayoress II
Owned/Bred: Mrs Mansfield

Merry Peeress — Bitch (C1890)
Ch.Boodles Esq x Ch.Lady Mayoress II

Merry's Son — White/Black dog (1898)

Midshipman — Black dog ((1932)
Ch.Brave Michael x Freya of Avalon

Midway Gipsy Seaolar of Perryhow — Black dog (1947)
Am.Ch.Millcreek Seafarer of Manitou x Am.Ch.Shelton Mermaid Queen Gipsy
Owned: Mrs M. Bennett/Bred: O.M.Daniels-Stobbart

Mill Boy or Milk Boy — White/Black dog (1902)
Steersman x Lady's Maid
Owned: Mrs Lindsay/Bred: Mr Mansfield

Mistress of the Robes — Bitch (1881)
Ch.Nelson II x Jennie
Owned: Mr Mansfield/Bred: Mrs E. Nichols

Molly of Dover — Bitch (1909)

Monarch of Heywood — Dog (1902)
Humber Sultan x

Dutch Ch.Monna Vanna del Serchio — Black bitch (C1926)
Ch.Siki x Southlands Pride

Mossie of Littlecreek — Black bitch (1963)
Littlecreeks Sea Pirate x Littlecreeks Sea Imp of Perryhow
Owned/Bred: Mr F. Cassidy

Nelson II — Black dog (1878)
Ch.Nep x Nancy
Owned: Mrs E. Nichols/Bred: Mrs Cunliffe-Lee

Nep — Dog (1873)
Atkinson's Cato x Joan
Owned/Bred: Mrs Cunliffe-Lee

Netherwood Donovan — Black dog (1929)
Ch.Black and White x Ch.Netherwood Queen
Bred: Mrs Dent

Netherwood Queen — Black bitch (1926)
Ch.Siki x Lady Mayco
Owned: Mrs Dent/Bred: Mrs McCann

SA.Ch.Pendragon Boltarson — Black dog (1974)
Greenayre Able-Seaman x SA.Ch.Plaisance Tillicum
Owned/Bred: Mr & Mrs Wilkins

'Pied in Crime of Esmeduna — Black dog (1967)
Isambard Hereward of Esmeduna x Ch.Storytime Black Pearl of Esmeduna
Owned: Mrs Poor/Bred: Mr C. Whittaker

Pirate King — Black dog (1888)
Ch.Courtier x probably Baroness
Owned: Mr Paterson/Bred: Mrs Cunliffe-Lee

Int.Ch.Plaisance Night Sentinel — Black dog (C1972)
Ch.Sigroc King Neptune x Sparry's Lively Lady of Plaisance
Owned: M.Engrand(France)/Bred: Mr T. McKenna

SA.Ch.Plaisance Tillicum — Black bitch (C1970)
Ch.Cascar Merikoira x Sparry's Lively Lady of Plaisance
Owned: Mrs P. Wilkins/Bred: Mr T. McKenna

President McKinley — White/Black dog (1901)
Lord Byron x probably Bonnie Lassie

Prince Charlie — Dog (1879)
Ch.Dick x Dinah
Owned/Bred: Mr G. Chapman

Prince of Norfolk — White/Black dog (1897)
Ch.His Nibs x Princess May II

Prince of Suffolk — White/Black dog (1903)
Ch.Prince of Norfolk x Lady's Maid
Owned: Mrs Grenville/Bred: Mr Mansfield

Prince Rudolph — Dog (1913)
Ch.Gipsy Duke x Cumberland Lassie
Owned/Bred: W. Hudson

Am.Ch.Princess Sonya — Black bitch (C1926)
Ch.Siki x Black Queen

Queenie — Bitch (C1900)
Ch.Wolf of Badenoch x Una
Owned: Mrs A.W. Jepson

Queen of Hearts — Black bitch (1923)
Ch.Ferrol Neptune x Queen Bess
Owned/Bred: Mrs C Roberts

Queen of the Roses — Bitch (1910)
Omega x Tylehurst Lassie
Owned: Mrs Wetwan/Bred: Mr Dickman

Queen of Surrey — Bitch
Owned: Mr van Weede

Ragtime Off She Trots — Black bitch (1972)
Ragtime Attimore Sirius x Skyro de la Mare Bleue
Owned: Mrs M. Eidson/Bred: Mr Alcock

Ravendale — Dog
Furness Roy x Walney Bell

Rosebud — White/Black bitch (C1885)
Ch.Trojan x Leda
Owned: Mr H.R.Farquharson, MP

Rothwell Bess — Black bitch (1919)
Ch.Gipsy Boy x Galphay Jess
Owned/Bred: Mr Bland

Sandown Ruler — Dog

Scout — Dog (1904)
Ch.Monarch of Heywood x Lady Seike
Owned: H.Pudsey/Bred: J. Partington

Sea Captain of Perryhow — Black dog (1952)
Ch.Midway Gipsy Seaolar of Perryhow x The Barribals Anca of Perryhow
Owned: F. Tishenden/Bred: Mrs M. Bennett

Seagrave Blackberry — Black bitch (1925)
Ch.Siki x Maori Girl
Owned/Bred: Mr Bland

Sea Gipsy of Perryhow — Black bitch (1953)
Ch.Midway Gipsy Seaolar of Perryhow x The Barribals Anca of Perryhow
Owned: Mrs G. Shapland/Bred: Mrs M. Bennett

Sea Lord of Sparry — Black dog (1954)
Nero of Sparry x Seanymph of Sparry
Owned: Mr & Mrs Aberdeen/Bred: Mr Aberdeen

Seanca of Perryhow — Black bitch (1958)
Beau of Sparry x Britannia of Verduron
Owned: Miss Elles/Bred: Mrs M. Bennett

Sea Nymph — Bitch
Owned: Mr Mansfield

Sea Shanty of Perryhow — Black bitch (1950)
Brave Serestus x The Barribals Anca of Perryhow
Owned/Bred: Mrs M Bennett

Sea Shell of Little Creek — Black bitch (1966)
Little Creek's Sea Pirate of Sparry x Little Creek's Sea Imp of Perryhow
Owned: Mrs Symes/Bred: Mr Cassidy

Sea Urchin of Sparry — Black dog (1954)
Nero of Sparry x Seanymph of Sparry
Owned: Mr F. Cassidy/Bred: Mrs Aberdeen

Sebastian of Middleham — Black dog (1934)
Sir Launcelot x Deborah the Prophetess
Owned/Bred: Miss Topham

Sheba of Sparry — Black bitch (1953)
Nero of Sparry x Seanymph of Perryhow
Owned: Mr & Mrs Lindley/Bred: Mrs Aberdeen

Can.Ch.Shelton Cabin Boy — Black dog (1926)
Ch.Siki x Harlingen Topsy
Bred: W. Bursey

Shelton Gipsy Lass — Black bitch (1922)
Ch.Gipsy Boy x Lady Mayco
Owned: Mrs Wetwan/Bred: Mrs McCann

Shelton King — Black dog (1917)
Gipsy Viscount x Mollie
Owned: Lt-Col Wetwan/Bred: Miss Goodall

Shelton Ruler — Black dog (C1906)
Ch.Shelton Viking x

Shelton Snowflake — See Lincoln Snowflake
Shelton Ursula — Bitch (1903)
Lord Rosebery x Shelton Madge

Shelton Viking — Black dog (1903)
Lord Rosebery x Shelton Madge
Owned/Bred: Mrs Wetwan

Sigroc King Neptune — Black dog (1967)
Harmonattan Okay x Marun Kiva
Owned: Miss Davies/Bred: Miss R. Friend

Sigroc Miss Me (JW) — Black bitch (1971)
Ch.Sigroc King Neptune x Ch.Merikarhun Fay of Sigroc
Owned/Bred: Miss J. Davies

SA.Ch.Sigroc Sir Percival — Black dog (1975)
Ch.Capt. Starlight of Littlegrange x Ch.Sigroc Miss Me
Owned: Mr & Mrs Wilkins/Bred: Miss Davies

Siki — Black dog (1922)
Ch.Shelton King x Ch.Rothwell Bess
Owned/Bred: Mr Bland

Am.Ch.Sonny Boy of Littlegrange — Black dog (1966)
Suleskerry Steersman x Ch.Cherry of Littlegrange
Bred: Mrs F. Warren

Sparry's Amphitrite of Fairwater — Black bitch (1975)
Patriot of Witchazel x Naze Snowdrop
Owned: Mr & Mrs Aberdeen/Bred: Mrs C. Handley

Int.Ch.Sparry's Treasure of Littlegrange — Black bitch (1966)
Suleskerry Steersman x Ch.Cherry of Littlegrange
Bred: Mrs Warren

Statesman — Black-and-tan dog

Stormsail Matterhorn (JW) — Black dog (1975)
Ch.Attimore Royal Sovereign x Ch.Bachalaos Bright Water of Stormsail
Owned/Bred: Mr & Mrs P. Oriani

NZ.Ch.Stormsail Rothorn — Black bitch (1975)
Ch.Attimore Royal Sovereign x Ch.Bachalaos Bright Water of Stormsail
Owned: Mr & Mrs A. Hooper/Bred: Mr & Mrs P. Oriani

Stormsail Wetterhorn (JW) — Black bitch (1975)
Ch.Attimore Royal Sovereign x Ch. Bachalaos Bright Water of Stormsail
Owned/Bred: Mr & Mrs P. Oriani

NZ.Ch.Stormsail Wildhorn — Black dog (1975)
Ch.Attimore Royal Sovereign x Ch.Bachalaos Bright Water of Stormsail
Owned: Mr & Mrs A. Hooper/Bred: Mr & Mrs P. Oriani

Storytime Black Pearl of Esmeduna — Black bitch (1965)
Suleskerry Steersman x Storytime Susan
Owned: Mr C. Whittaker/Bred: Mrs Henry

Storytime Whaler — Black dog (1962)
Sailorboy of Verduron x Storytime Snowshoes
Owned/Bred: Mrs Henry

Suisseberne Sealore of Perryhow — Black bitch (1950)
Brave Serestus x The Barribals Anca of Perryhow
Owned: Mrs Mason/Bred: Mrs Bennett

Sukiln Polly Wagtail — Black bitch (1973)
Ch.Sigroc King Neptune x Gentle Lady of Littlegrange
Owned/Bred: Miss E. Osmond

Sybil — Bitch
Owned: Mrs Mansfield

Tarnhill Sound of Arisaig (JW) — Black dog (1972)
Black Chieftain x Storm Wind
Owned: Mrs Powell/Bred: Mrs Taylor

Ta-Ta Maria of Littlegrange — Black bitch (1972)
Ch.Captain Starlight of Littlegrange x Sea-Shanty of Littlegrange
Owned/Bred: Mrs J. Warren

The Black Prince — (see Black Prince)
Theodore Nero — Black dog (1868)
breeding unknown — whelped in St. John's
Owned: Dr Gordon Stables

Thornhill Rival — Bitch (1904)
Ch.Humber Jumbo x Humber Gem
Owned: W. Shearer-Clarke/Bred: Mr Haldenby

Timbuctoo — Black dog (1916)
Gipsy Baronet x Queen of Durham
Owned: Mr Graham/Bred: Mr J.T. Dent

Trafalgar — White/Black dog (1879)
Nelson x Empress
Owned/Bred: Mr H.R. Farquharson, MP

Trojan — Black dog (1881)
Viceroy x Lady Beaconsfield
Owned/bred: Mr. H.R. Farquharson, MP

Dutch Ch.Uncle Tom Detto Maso — Black dog (1929 or 30)
Ch.Brave Michael x Judith van de Negerhut
Bred: Miss V.H. Deane

Uskrail Faroes — Black dog (1970)
Ragtime Attimore Sirius x Uskrail Kentish Anne
Owned: Mr D. Jeffries/Bred: Miss Chadwick

Aus.Ch.Wanitopa Bosun Boy — Black dog (1969)
Aus.Ch.Wanitopa Gentle Giant x Aus.&.Eng.Ch.Bonnybay Jasmine
Owned: Miss McCaul/Bred: Mrs J. Gibson

Eng.&.Aus.Ch.Wanitopa Comedy — White/black bitch (1969)
Aus.Ch.Wanitopa Gentle Giant x Eng.&.Aus.Ch.Bonnybay Jasmine
Owned/Bred: Mrs J. Gibson

Aus.Ch.Wanitopa Gentle Giant — Black dog (1965)
Suleskerry Steersman x Dory'os Harbour Grace
Owned/Bred: Mrs J. Gibson

Wanitopa Matilda — Black bitch (1969)
Aus.Ch.Wanitopa Gentle Giant x Eng.&.Aus.Ch.Bonnybay Jasmine
Owned: Mrs Nix/Bred: Mrs J. Gibson

Waterbaby — Dog

Water Rat — Black dog (1930)
Ch.Brave Michael x Judith van de Negerhut
Owned: Mr H.S. Gunn/Bred: Miss V.H. Deane

Waterwitch — Black bitch (1920)
Ch.Sandown Ruler x Ch.Rothwell Bess
Owned: Mr Brand/Bred: Mr. Bland

Welsh Nell — White/Black bitch (1881)

White Squall — White/Black dog (1887)
New Clee Lion x Ch.Welsh Nell

Wolf of Badenoch — Black dog (1893)
Ch.Pirate King x King's Topsy
Owned: Mrs Ingleton

Woodlesfield Gem — Bitch (1907)
Omega x Lady Dorothy
Owned: H.Sheldon/Bred: Mr F. Fearn

Woodlesfield Pioneer — Dog (1910)
Ch.Prince of Suffolk x Ch. Woodlesfield Gem
Owned/Bred: H. Sheldon

Your Sweet Bippy of Esmeduna — Black bitch (1969)
Avalons Ikaros of Littlegrange x A Maiden Tender of Esmeduna
Owned: Mrs J. Warren/Bred: Mr C. Whittaker

Zingari Chief — Black dog (1910)
Ch.Gipsy Duke x Lady Melbourne
Owned: Mr Mansfield/Bred: Mr W. Parker

Zoë — Black bitch (1878)
Robson's Leo x Lady Sarah
Owned: Mrs Mansfield/Bred: C. Dennis

JUNIOR WARRANT HOLDERS

Ch.Sigroc Miss Me
(Ch.Sigroc King Neptune x Ch.Merikarhun Fay of Sigroc)
Owned & Bred: Miss J.M. Davies

Ch.Tarnhill Sound of Arisaig
(Black Chieftain x Storm Wind)
Owned: Mrs E. Powell/Bred: Mrs E. Taylor

Sea Clipper of Littlegrange
(Avalon's Ikaros of Littlegrange x Harlingen Curlew)
Owned: Mr & Mrs Raczycki/Bred: A & C Clarke

Esmeduna's Happy Result of Orovales
(Ch.Sigroc King Neptune x Ch.I'm Dimpy Too of Esmeduna)
Owned: Miss Yeoward/Bred: Mr C Whittaker

Esmeduna's Old Chum of Mine
(Breeding as above)
Owned: Mrs and Miss Crackle

Ch.Stormsail Matterhorn
(Ch.Attimore Royal Sovereign x Ch.Bachalaos Bright Water of Stormsail)
Owned/Bred: Mr & Mrs P. Oriani

Ch.Stormsail Wetterhorn
(Breeding as above)
Owned/Bred: Mr & Mrs P. Oriani

Appendix III

Avalon's Ikaros of Littlegrange — Black dog (1966)
Nattanin Ralli x Avalon's Castalia
Bred: Mrs A.G.P. van Zijl (Holland)/Owned: Mrs J. Warren

The Barribals Anca of Perryhow — Black bitch (1948)
Alex von Froonacker x Fiesta v.d. Oldehove
Bred: Mr Tempel (Holland)/Owned: Mrs M Bennett

Big Skys Love You Valentine of Littlecreek — Black bitch (1974)
Can.Ch.Little Bears Geminis Boy x Big Skys Harry Easter
Bred: S. Payne (U.S.A.)/Owned: Mr F. Cassidy

Dory O'S Harbour Grace — Black bitch (1959)
Wizard of Oz x Glenmire Governor's Lady
Bred:Mrs Cochrane (Canada)/Owned: (1) Mrs A.Cooper (2) Mrs J. 'Gibson

Gipsy von Heidenberg of Harraton — Landseer bitch (1974)
Allan von Heidenberg x Carmen von Heidenberg
Bred: P Müller (Germany)/Owned: Mr K. Frost

Harlingen Taaran Taru — Landseer bitch (1964)
Gerogeest Domino x Fin. Ch.Taaran Rita
Bred: Miss Jaaskelainen (Finland)/Owned: Mrs C. Roberts

Harlingen Waseeka's Black Gold — Black bitch (1946)
Sheena Lynnwoods Man O'War x Dinah Magnus
Bred: W.M.Magnusson (U.S.A.)/Owned: Mrs C. Roberts

Harmonattan Okay — Black dog (1960)
Fin.Ch.Gerogeest Attan x Fin.Ch.Norma's Harmonia
Bred: Mr Solantra (Finland)/Owned: Mr W.M. Morgan

Kumletaras — Black dog (1976)
Int.&.Dan.Ch.Kaniz Major Skibber x Hennessy
Bred: in Denmark/Owned: Mrs Blackman

Lancelot of Shermead — Black dog (1974)
Dutch.Ch.Ristolahden Cogi x Dutch Ch. Jolly
Bred: Mrs E. Hounskola (Holland)/Owned: Mr & Mrs J. Adey

Lasso von der Weilerhöhe of Harraton — Landseer dog (1972)
Herakles v.d. Boberburg x Edda v.d.Weilerhöhe
Bred:Herr Miller (Germany)/Owned: Mr K. Frost

Little Bears Geni of Littlecreek — Black bitch (1973)
Little Bears Fishing Admiral x Little Bears Pride of the Morn
Bred: Little Bear Kennels (U.S.A.)/Owned: Mr F. Cassidy

Little Bears Scannon of Littlecreek — Black dog (1972)
Little Bears Two if by Sea x Little Bears Oh How She Scoones
Bred: Little Bear Kennels (U.S.A.)/Owned: Mr F. Cassidy

Marun Kiva — Black bitch (1964)
Merikarhun Caius x Taara Jaija
Bred: Mrs Ruskeala (Finland)/Owned: Miss Friend

Ch.Merikarhun Fay of Sigroc — Black bitch (1966)
Fin.Ch.Alderbay Attila x Fin.Ch.Merikarhun Desire
Bred: J. Salminen (Finland)/Owned: Miss J.M. Davies

Midian Dryad's Sea Anchor — Black dog (1955)
Am.Ch.Dryad's Pilot x Waseeka's Harbour Light
Bred: Mrs K Drury (U.S.A.)/Owned: Mrs Pat Handley

Ch.Midway Gipsy Seaolar of Perryhow — Black bitch (1947)
Am.Ch.Millcreek Seafarer of Manitou x Am.Ch.Shelton Mermaid Gipsy Queen
Bred: Mrs O.M.Daniels-Stobbart (U.S.A.)/Owned: Mrs M. Bennett

Naze Troll von Schartenberg — Landseer dog (1953)
Alberic v.d.Lüneberger Heide x Olla von Schartenberg
Bred: Mr O. Walterspiel (Germany)/Owned: Mr D. Blyth

Seawards Pride of America — Landseer bitch (1975)
Seawards Obiter Dictum x Seawards Flying Cloud
Bred: N. Ayers (U.S.A.)/Owned: Mr Blyth & Mrs Handley

Shadfields Lucky Boy of Wanitopa — Black dog (1968)
Am.Ch.Thelma's Boy CD x Am.Ch.Schooner's Black Phantom
Bred: Mrs Basterfield (U.S.A.)/Owned: Mrs J. Gibson

Shadfields Rutherford House of Wanitopa — Black dog (1968)
Am.Ch.Thelma's Boy CD x Am.Ch.Schooner's Black Phantom
Bred: Mrs Basterfield (U.S.A.)/Owned: Mrs Beats

Shermead Bijou of the Thatched Roof — Black bitch (1974)
Shermead Lively Lad x Atania v.d.Zonne Dauw
Bred: Mr Doremalen (Holland)/Owned: Mr & Mrs J. Adey

Skyro de la Mare Bleue — Black bitch (1969)
Niko de la Mare Bleue x Naloue de la Mare Bleue
Bred: Mme Ravise (France)/Owned: Mr G. Alcock

Suleskerry Seawards Sea Billow — Landseer bitch
Montana Bandit Arno x Dryads Blanca Sultana
Bred: N. Ayers (U.S.A.)/Owned: Miss I. Morrison

Terra Nova Homer — Black dog (1966)
Can.Ch.Edenglen's Black Sambo x Dory O's Top This
Bred: Mr H.W. Duffett (Canada)/Owned: Dr. Knight

Aus.&.Eng.Ch.Wanitopa Comedy — Landseer bitch (1969)
Aus.Ch.Wanitopa Gentle Giant x Aus.&.Eng.Ch.Bonnybay Jasmine
Owned/Bred: Mrs J. Gibson (Australia)

Appendix IV

GENERAL INFORMATION

1. **A list of Shows currently scheduling Newfoundland Classes (dates are approximate)**

January	City of Bristol (Limited)
February	Crufts (Championship) — Challenge Certificates
March	Club Open Show
April	Hammersmith Canine Society (Open)
	West of England Ladies Kennel Society (Championship) — Challenge Certificates
May	Bath Canine Society (Championship) — Challenge Certificates
	Birmingham National (Championship) — Challenge Certificates
	Scottish Kennel Club — Edinburgh (Championship) — Challenge Certificates
	Guildford Canine Society (Open)
	Leeds (Championship) — Challenge Certificates
	Bristol Canine Society (Open)
June	Bath and West (Open)
	Blackpool (Championship) — Challenge Certificates
July	Windsor (Championship) — No Challenge Certificates
	Clacton and District Canine Society (Open)
	East of England — Peterborough (Championship) — Challenge Certificates
	Border Union Agricultural Society (Championship) — Challenge Certificates
August	Newfoundland Club Water Trials and Rally — Alcester
	Welsh Kennel Club — Builth Wells (Championship) — Challenge Certificates
	Scottish Kennel Club — Glasgow (Championship) — Challenge Certificates
	Poole and District Canine Society (Open)
	Leicester City Canine Society (Championship) — Challenge Certificates
September	City of Birmingham (Championship) — Challenge Certificates
	Brent — North London (Open)
	National Working Breeds (Championship) — Challenge Certificates
October	Ladies Kennel Association (Championship) — Challenge Certificates
November	**Newfoundland Club Show — Stonleigh (Championship) — Challenge Certificates**

2. The Title of Champion

A dog may be called a Champion, if he has won three challenge Certificates under three different judges. One of these certificates must have been won after the dog reached twelve months of age.

Not all show societies which schedule Newfoundlands automatically offer Challenge Certificates, even though they may have Championship status. The allocation of certificates rests with the Kennel Club. Broadly speaking, it is based on annual registration figures taken from the previous three years before the year of allocation. However, the system is at present under review, and it seems likely that in future the allotment of certificates will be geared in some way to the numbers of dogs being exhibited, as well as registrations. Certificates have been allocated for 1977, so there is no possibility of a change from the present system until at least 1978.

3. The Junior Warrent

The Junior Warrent is awarded to dogs which have won twenty-five points at championship and open shows, while still under the age of eighteen months.

The points are awarded as follows: —

(a) For each First Prize in a breed class at a championship show at which Challenge Certificates are offered for the breed . . . 3 points

(b) For each First Prize in a breed class at a championship show where Challenge Certificates are **not** offered, or at an open show . . . 1 point

A class open to more than one variety of a breed is not a breed class. Only the registered owner at the time of qualification may apply. The Junior Warrent is not awarded automatically and the owner should claim it by application to the Kennel Club, giving details of the wins concerned.

4. Addresses

The Chairman of the Newfoundland Club:
Mr C. Whittaker,
Tower View,
Hardway,
Bruton,
Somerset   Telephone: Bruton 2299

The secretary of the Newfoundland Club:
Miss J.M. Davies,
Old Shelve Farm,
Lenham,
Maidstone,
Kent.   Telephone: Lenham 269

The treasurer of the Newfoundland Club:
Mrs J. Warren,
Froglands Cross Farm,
Winterbourne,
Bristol BS17 1RU, Avon.   Telephone: 0454-778457

The Kennel Club,
1 Clarges Street,
Piccadilly,
London, W1Y 8AB
                                             Telephone: 01-493 6651

BIBLIOGRAPHY

ALLEN, Glover M. — "Dog Skulls from Uyak Bay, Kodiak Island" (Jour.Mam. vol. 20 1939)

ALLEN, Glover M. — "Dogs of the American Aborigines" (Bull.Mus.Comp.Zool. 1920).

ASH, Edward C. — "Dogs, their History and Development" (London 1927).

BALLANTYNE, R.M. — "The Dog Crusoe: a Tale of the Western Prairie" (Blackie and Son 1832).

BEAMISH, DOCKERILL & HILLIER — "The Pride of Poole" (Town and Country of Poole 1974).

BEWICK, Thomas. — "A General History of Quadrupeds" (Newcastle-upon-Tyne 1807)

BLAIN, Delabere P. — "An Encyclopaedia of Rural Sports" (London 1875).

BLUNDEN, Edmund. — "Poems of Spirit and Adventure"

BOUDET. — "Man and Beast". (Bodley Head 1964).

BOOTH CHERN, Margaret. — "The Complete Newfoundland" (Howell Co 1976)

BRINKLEY, Mrs. M. — Personal Communication

COMPTON, H.E. — "The Twentieth Century Dog"

CROXTON-SMITH, A. — "About Our Dogs" (Ward Lock and Co Ltd 1931)

CROXTON-SMITH, A. — "British Dogs at Work" (London 1906)

CROXTON-SMITH, A. — "Everyman's Book of the Dog" (Hodder and Stoughton 1909)

DALZIEL, Hugh. — "British Dogs" (L.Upcott Gill 1889)

DANIEL, William Barker. — "Rural Sports" Vol. 1

DRURY/LINN — "How to Raise and Train a Newfoundland" (T.F.H.Publications, USA 1964)

DRURY, Mrs M.K. (Edited) — "The is the Newfoundland" 2nd Edition (T.F.H.Publications, Inc., 1969)

EDWARDS, Mrs F.V. — Personal Communication

EDWARDS, Sydenham. — "Cynographia Britannica" (1800)

FIENNES — "The Natural History of the Dog"

GOLDSMITH, Oliver — "Animated Nature" Vol 1 (A.Fullarton & Co 1856 — first published C1790)

GRAY, John E. — "Notes on the Skulls of the Species of Dogs, Wolves and Foxes in the Collection of the British Museum" (Proc.Zoo.Soc.Lond. 1868)

HAMILTON-SMITH, Charles — "Dogs" Vol II (Jardin's Naturalists Library, Edinburgh 1840)

HATTON & M.HARVEY — "Newfoundland" (Doyle and Whittle 1883)

HEIM, Dr Albert. — "Der Neufundlanderhund" (Switzerland 1937)

HUBBARD, C.L.B. — "Dogs in Britain" (1948)

HUBBARD, C.L.B. — "The Literature of British Dogs" (1949)

HUBBARD, C.L.B. — "Working Dogs of the World" (Sidgwich and Jackson 1947)

HUTCHINSON, Gen W.N. – "Dog Breaking" (John Murray 1909)

HUTCHINSON, Gen W.N. – "Dog Breeding" 6th Edition (1909)

HUTCHINSON'S DOG ENCYCLOPAEDIA – (Hutchinson and Co 1934)

IDSTONE – "The Dog (1872)

JESSE, G.R. – "Anecdotes of Dogs" (C1860)

JESSE, G.R. – "Researches into the History of the British Dog" (Robert Hardwicke 1866)

KANE, Dr Elisha Kent – "Arctic Expedition" – 2 vols (Philadelphia 1856)

LAROUSSE ILLUSTREE – (France, C1921)

LAWRENCE Richard – "The Complete Farrier and British Sportsman" (1816)

LEE, Rawden B. – "Modern Dogs" (Horace Cox 1893)

LEIGHTON, Robert – "The New Book of the Dog" (London 1907)

MACPHERSON, The Hon Harold – "The Newfoundland Dog" (Richard Clay & Sons Ltd., 1937)

"The Gentleman Farrier" (London 1878)

MARCHAND, Leslie A. – 'Byron – a Portrait" (Murray 1957)

MERLEN, Rene Henry Albert – "De Canibus" (J.A.Allen & Co Ltd)

MEYRICK, John – "House Dogs and Sporting Dogs" (London 1861)

MORRISON, Miss I. – Personal Communication

MURIE, Olaus J. – "Dogs of the Arctic Frontier" (Nature Mag. 1925)

MURIE, Olaus J. – "Dog Skulls from Ipiutak" (Anthropos. Papers.Amer.Mus.Nat.Hist. 1948)

"The Book of Dogs" (Nat. Geog.Mag. 1927)

NUTBEAM, Mrs Megan – "The Newfoundland" (Article published 1967)

PACKARD, A.S. – "Origin of the American Varieties of the Dog" (Amer.Nat. 1885)

PEARCE, Thomas – "The Dog" (London 1872)

PIETERSE, Johan – "The Newfoundland – How he lives and is bred" (Amsterdam 1937)

PURDY, Donn M. – "Living with your Newfoundland Dog" (Ontario 1971)

RICHARDSON, Col E.H. – "British War Dogs"

ROBINSON, Lt-Col R.B. – Personal Communication

SANDERSON C.C. – "Pedigree Dogs"

SHAW, Vero – "The Illustrated Book of the Dog" (Cassel, Peter Galpin & Co 1881)

SKINNER, J.S. – "The Dog and the Sportsman" (Philadelphia 1824 or 1845)

SMALLWOOD, J.R. – "The Book of Newfoundland" (Newfoundland Pub.Ltd., St. John's 1937)

STABLES, Dr Gordon – "Ladies' Dogs as Companions" (London 1879)

STABLES, Dr Gordon – "Our Friend the Dog" (Dean and son 1889)

STABLES, Dr Gordon – "The Practical Kennel Guide" (C1883)

STETSON, Joe (edited) – "This is the Newfoundland" 1st Edition (Practical Science Pub. Co. Inc. 1956)

STONEHENGE (J.H.Walsh) – "British Rural Sports" (F.Warne & Co 1855)

STONEHENGE (J.H.Walsh) — "The Dog" (1887)

STONEHENGE (J.H.Walsh) — "Dogs of the British Isles" ("Field" Office, London, 1878)

STONEHENGE (J.H.Walsh) — "The Dogs of Great Britain, America and Other Countries" (New York 1880)

STONEX, Mrs E. — Personal Communication

SYMES, Mrs Diana — Personal Communication

TAPLIN, W. — "The Sportsman's Cabinet" (1803-4)

TOPSELL — "History of the Foure-footed Beastes" (1607)

VESEY-FITZGERALD, Brian — "The Book of the Dog" (Routledge, Kegan Paul 1946)

WATSON, James — "The Dog Book" (Doubleday 1920)

WENTWORTH-DAY, James — "The Dog in Sport"

YOUATT, William — "The Dog" (London 1845)

YOUNG, Stanley — "What was the Early Indian Dog?" (Amer.Forests Washington DC, Vol 49-50. 1943-44)

ZEUNER, Frederick E. — "A History of Domesticated Animals" (Hutchinson 1963)

INDEX

185

Printed by Mid-Wales Litho Limited, Crickhowell.